W9-ARS-239

Start & Run a

Marijuana Dispensary or Pot Shop

Wherever It Is Legal

Jay Currie

Self-Counsel Press
(a division of)
International Self-Counsel Press Ltd.
Canada   USA

Self-Counsel Press acknowledges the financial support of the Government of Canada through the Canada Book Fund (CBF) for our publishing activities.

Printed in Canada.

First edition: 2016

Library and Archives Canada Cataloguing in Publication

Currie, Jay, 1956-, author

    Start & run a marijuana dispensary or pot shop : wherever it is legal / Jay Currie.

(Self-counsel business series)
Includes bibliographical references and index.
Issued in print and electronic formats.
ISBN 978-1-77040-262-1 (paperback).—ISBN 978-1-77040-470-0 (epub).— ISBN 978-1-77040-471-7 (kindle)

    1. Marijuana industry. 2. Marijuana—Law and legislation. 3. Dispensaries. 4. New business enterprises. I. Title. II. Title: Start and run a marijuana dispensary or pot shop. III. Title: Marijuana dispensary or pot shop. IV. Series: Self-Counsel business series

HD9019.M38C87 2016   381'.41379   C2016-905144-7
                                                        C2016-905145-5

MIX
Paper from
responsible sources
FSC® C004071

Self-Counsel Press
(a division of)
International Self-Counsel Press Ltd.

North Vancouver, BC   Bellingham, WA
Canada   USA

Contents

Notice to Readers

Laws are constantly changing. Every effort is made to keep this publication as current as possible. However, the author, the publisher, and the vendor of this book make no representations or warranties regarding the outcome or the use to which the information in this book is put and are not assuming any liability for any claims, losses, or damages arising out of the use of this book. The reader should not rely on the author or the publisher of this book for any professional advice. Please be sure that you have the most recent edition.

Website links often expire or web pages move; at the time of this book's publication the links were current.

Acknowledgments

My eldest son Simon pretty much wrote the chapter on Marijuana 101. I thank him for his insights and his willingness to bring his aged father's pot knowledge up to date. My younger sons, Sam and Max, put up with their father's retailing of silly marijuana regulations at the dinner table and feigned interest in discussions of the declining marijuana margins in states with legal pot.

Linda Richards, my friend and publisher, went to bat for this book and simply assumed that, of course, I could write a book.

My sweet Susan has held my hand and kept her pretty eyes at least partially open as I blathered on about pot. Her patience and support are my strength. I am lucky to know her.

Introduction:
The Green Rush
and You

All over North America, the politics of marijuana have reached the tipping point. Whether it is the legalization of marijuana for medical use, the licensing of medical marijuana dispensaries, or the legalization of marijuana for recreational use, marijuana is entering the legal mainstream.

As the law changes, businesspeople have seen opportunities and entered the marijuana marketplace. Researchers from The ArcView Group, a cannabis industry investment and research firm based in Oakland, California, found that the US market for legal cannabis grew 74 percent in 2014 to $2.7 billion USD, up from $1.5 billion in 2013. As more states legalize either medical or recreational marijuana, ArcView projects the US marijuana market will expand to an $11 billion USD a year industry by 2019. In Canada, despite a regulatory disaster on the medical marijuana side, the authorized medical marijuana market is between $80–$100 million CAD. If, as promised, the federal government legalizes recreational use, the overall market in that country is estimated to be worth up to $5 billion a year.

These are big numbers. Billionaire investors such as PayPal cofounder Peter Thiel are putting multimillion-dollar bets on companies in the space. Thiel's partner Geoff Lewis understands something which, in many ways, is the theme of this book: "We're fine with investing in businesses with regulatory ambiguity, because we believe that regulation follows public sentiment."

Unlike many of the businesses a person can start, the marijuana business is driven by demand on one side and regulation on the other. As a potential marijuana business owner you will be trying to meet the demand for marijuana products while, at the same time, complying with the regulatory regime in your particular jurisdiction. It's a balancing act.

This balancing act can be complicated by what is essentially an artificial, but legally important, distinction between medical and recreational pot usage. Back in the days of Prohibition there was a similar distinction. "For medical use only" allowed doctors to prescribe brandy or other alcohol to particular patients. As you might guess, alcohol quickly became the medication of choice for all manner of minor ailments.

For marijuana activists, medical marijuana was, and is, politically, a way forward in the campaign to legalize pot. Proposition 215 in California led to the Compassionate Use Act of 1996 which allowed people suffering from AIDS, cancer, and other chronic illnesses to grow or obtain marijuana when recommended by a doctor. Subsequent amendments to that law and its regulations has led to a widening of the exemptions created in 1996. The introduction of a medical marijuana user identification card in 2003 streamlined, to a degree, the medical marijuana regulation system in that state. Versions of the California system have been implemented in a dozen other states.

There are two key facts about medical marijuana in US states: First, there is very limited evidence of marijuana's medical efficacy. While there is plenty of anecdotal evidence that marijuana has a positive effect on everything from cancer to sleeplessness, the hard core, double-blind evidence is limited. Second, marijuana remains illegal under federal law regardless of why it is being used. Where a state has legalized pot for medical or recreational purposes, the present federal position is that it will not prosecute unless there is evidence of organized criminal involvement but, as we'll see, continuing illegality creates a lot of regulatory ambiguity.

Using the legalization of medical marijuana as a political wedge has been very effective, however, it creates more than a little confusion for a businessperson thinking about entering the marijuana market. Will he or she have to set up as a medical marijuana dispensary? Or is it possible in the jurisdiction to set up as a recreational pot shop? Here, at least, the laws and regulations in each state are unambiguous: Unless recreational marijuana is expressly legal in your state — Washington, Colorado, Oregon, Alaska, and DC at time of writing — you cannot set up recreationally.

The regulatory situation in the US is a bit confusing, however, state by state the regulatory situation is quite clear. This is in sharp contrast to Canada which we'll take a closer look at later on, but for a businessperson the state of Canadian regulation is more than a little difficult. Put simply, there is a medical marijuana regulation scheme in place, but its operation has been halted by a federal court case. That case was recently decided but has left the situation just as murky because the judge ruled that the current regulations were not fit for constitutional purpose, and gave the Federal Government six months to come up with new ones. The Federal Government announced its new medical marijuana regulations August 11, 2016. Basically, registered users may grow a limited amount of pot for their own use and they can have someone grow their pot for them. No provision was made for "dispensaries."

This pretty much leaves a free-for-all in the medical space with dispensaries — not authorized under the regulatory scheme — being ignored by law enforcement in some areas and prosecuted in others. On the recreational side, the new government came in on a platform of legalization and regulation but it is all taking time to implement. Plus, in fine Canadian fashion, it is not at all obvious that the federal government, rather than the various provincial and municipal governments, is responsible for regulating the pot industry once marijuana has been legalized. There are ways forward for businesses but "regulatory ambiguity" barely begins to describe the Canadian situation.

Many Canadian marijuana entrepreneurs aren't waiting for the legal dust to settle and Parliament to legalize recreational use. A growing grey market of medical marijuana storefront dispensaries has sprung up in major Canadian cities. These retail operations were largely ignored by law enforcement until late May, 2016 in Toronto when the police raided 43 medical marijuana dispensaries, arrested 90 people, and laid 186 criminal charges.

People are attracted to the marijuana business for a variety of reasons. Some are passionate advocates for the medicinal benefits of pot; others see marijuana as a matter of liberty; still others want to ride the rising tide of opportunity marijuana is creating. This book, and its author, are entirely agnostic as to the medical and/or spiritual benefits of marijuana, and while the politics of legalization have implications for the risk profile of a marijuana-based business, they are only one of a set of variables a businessperson needs to assess. What this book is attempting to do is help its reader consider the business prospects of a marijuana business and provide a basic guide to opening such a business in the US or Canada.

Cannabis, Marijuana, or Pot?

In various jurisdictions "cannabis," which is the name of the genus of a flowering plant some of whose subspecies contain the psychoactive chemical tetrahydrocannabinol (THC), is referred to as marijuana for legal purposes. For many in the medical marijuana community, "cannabis" is the preferred term because of its scientific connotations. "Marijuana" is a more colloquial term and, for various reasons, is sometimes seen as somehow slighting or derogatory. "Pot" — and the many other slang terms for cannabis — is used all the time informally but generally in business a degree of formality is appropriate.

Dispensary, Pot Shop, Compassion Club, Cannabis Center?

When medical marijuana first emerged in the 1990s, a lot of the activity operated as compassion clubs or dispensaries. The term itself has no special legal significance, although in medical situations, it can denote an in-house pharmacy in a hospital or other care facility. The key thing was that "dispensary" sounded medical but did not get the medical marijuana people in trouble with the private pharmacies in their areas. Over time, the word has come to designate both medical marijuana and recreational marijuana stores. However, in jurisdictions where recreational pot has become legalized, stores tend to be called everything from pot shops to cannabis centers.

☙ ☙ ☙

Deciding to go into the marijuana retail business is like deciding to go into any other business but with a few extra wrinkles not experienced by something like a pet food store or a corner grocery. In every jurisdiction where medical or recreational marijuana has been legalized, it is also regulated. In many of those jurisdictions it is regulated to the point where a relatively simple retail store has to have a secure, lossless, complicated system to account for every 1/100th of a gram of product it sells. Plus, to avoid having criminals enter the legal business, there are stringent licensing requirements as to ownership and financing on both the medical and recreational sides.

This book is designed to give readers a broad overview of the retail marijuana business. First, all business is about a balance of risk versus reward. Minimizing risk while maximizing reward is the obvious, but sometimes overlooked equation for business success. Taking time to research and plan your business is a critical first step in solving that business equation. The more you know the more you can quantify and plan your way around the risks inherent in any business and, particularly, the marijuana business.

Second, in a regulated business you absolutely need a smart, knowledgeable, experienced lawyer. While you can and should read your jurisdiction's laws and regulations, a lawyer understands and can find out how that mass of words actually will affect the setup and day-to-day operations of your business. Good lawyers are expensive but getting excellent legal advice, particularly as you are setting up, will save you lots of money down the road. You will also benefit from the advice of a marijuana-savvy accountant.

Third, this book suggests you do a good deal of rigorous self-assessment and planning before you go into the marijuana business. In any business such planning is a key to success. In the marijuana business it is even more important because it will allow you to identify and deal with issues unique to the regulation of marijuana before you even apply for your license. The time you invest now will make the whole process more smooth and, if you get the license, will ensure that your marijuana business has every chance of success.

Finally, this book is not about the intricacies of growing marijuana or discussions of which varietals or strains a dispensary or pot shop should stock. Different business models ranging from "seed to sale" operations to artisanal recreational pot shops on a microbrewery model are all potentially viable. Creating an easy guide to the essentials of building your vision of a marijuana business is the aim of this book.

At the same time, the analysis in this book is deliberately hard-headed. While there is certainly a Green Rush going on, in many states the medical marijuana business is well established and there is significant competition. In states where recreational marijuana has been legalized there has been a well-funded rush to open pot shops under the new regulations. In the Canadian world of unclear regulations and selective police enforcement, medical marijuana dispensaries are popping up like mushrooms after a rain.

For a budding marijuana retail entrepreneur, rigorous and realistic analysis of the state of the marijuana market in your locality, the rules and regulations in your jurisdiction, and the Cost of Goods Sold (COGS) in your circumstances will make the difference between business success and failure.

In the next few years there will be many changes in the marijuana industry. In the US there is a good chance that the difficulties with banking revenue from marijuana businesses will be resolved. There is also a good chance that the IRS's current punitive view of the marijuana industry will be revised. More states will legalize recreational marijuana use and, as that happens, more states where marijuana is altogether prohibited will allow medical marijuana sales. It is a slow process but, in general, regulation does follow public sentiment. In Canada, a path to general legalization and regulation is likely to emerge from the current hodge-podge of legally failed regulation and prosecutorial and police discretion.

Normalization brings its own challenges to marijuana business models. Most importantly, it changes the risk profile of the business which, in turn, tends to reduce the margins available to marijuana growers and retailers.

Creating a successful marijuana business requires that you understand and properly analyze the risks inherent in your jurisdiction and plan and build your business accordingly. I hope this book will give you the tools you need to create a profitable marijuana business.

A Quick
Self-Assessment

People like you go into business every day. Whether it is with a franchise or a boutique or online concept, millions of people every year go into business for themselves. Some do it on the spur of the moment. Others research, plan, read books like this one, scout locations, and price stock-in-trade, all before sitting down to write a complete business plan and raising the money to cover the costs of opening and the first, predictably lean, years of operation. It would be nice if virtue was rewarded and it often is, but even hard work and great preparation is no guarantee of success.

Many people who go into business for themselves will tell you that they have never worked harder in their lives. If you are the owner there is no one else in charge, and unless you hire people, no one to take up the slack, or open the shop when you are sick. You do all the work, you keep all the profits — if any.

Not all the businesses people go into are retail — that is, selling something, usually a product, to the public. Retailing is seldom a good fit for shy or introverted people because, every day, people are going to walk through your door and want to be served. They will have questions. They will have complaints and concerns, and some will be downright annoying.

The legal marijuana business has its own challenges. Laws and regulations, security, the nature of the product, a whole world of knowledge, possibly the

requirement to actually grow an often finicky plant, and competition: There is a lot to do and a lot to know.

Setting up in the marijuana retail business requires planning, good legal and accounting advice, and start-up and operating funding.

This chapter is intended to make you take a realistic look at your strengths and weaknesses as a potential marijuana entrepreneur. There are no right answers and there are no answers which absolutely disqualify you — except the criminal record issue and even that may have solutions. Instead, these questions will focus your attention on whether you should work towards opening a marijuana retail dispensary or store.

1. Who Are You?

Everywhere medical or recreational marijuana has been legalized, the regulatory regime has been set up to try and keep "undesirable" elements out of the business. The systems, discussed further on, rely on a licensing process which is focused on the background of the people seeking the license. Your lawyer will walk you through your jurisdiction's requirements but the background checks are extensive and invasive. (In this era of really big and complete databases it is very tough to hide much ... so don't.)

1.1 Criminal record?

There is a perception that the various licensing authorities involved in the marijuana business will not license a person with a criminal record. While this may be the case in your jurisdiction, it likely isn't.

The Washington State regulation is a good example: The Board conducts a criminal record check on an applicant for a license. It scores a person's criminal record on a point system and if you get more than 8 points you will not normally be granted a license. But looking at the table of points, you quickly discover that even a full felony conviction, while it carries 12 points, only carries those points for ten years. So that conviction in 2003 does not, in fact, count against you as of this writing.

So the preliminary question is "Do you have any criminal convictions?" But then you have to go on to say, how serious was the offence and how long ago did it occur? As well, less serious misdemeanor offences may even be expunged from your record before you make an application for a license.

1.2 Employment

Background checks for licenses usually ask for employment history and having such a history is important. Of course, on the one hand, many people who are entrepreneurial enough to want to go into the retail marijuana business will tend to have been self-employed or doing contract work for several years. This is not likely to matter but it is worthwhile to walk through your employment history going back at least ten years or to the last educational institution attended, and put a date beside each job, contract, or business. For each, have at least one reference with contact details.

On the other hand, being employed and having a steady income before you embark on the marijuana journey is a very good idea. Licensing can take months, and it can take more months before your marijuana business opens its doors, and more months after that before you can take home a dollar. Having a secure income as long as possible is simply smart business.

1.3 Spouse or partner

Various jurisdictions have differing rules regarding spousal involvement in your marijuana business. A good example is Colorado which states in its eligibility for license criteria: "May not employ, be assisted by or financed in whole or in part by any other person whose criminal history indicates he or she is not of good character and reputation"; lawyers make good livings interpreting language like this. The reality is that if you are married to a person who has a felony conviction for a Controlled Substances offence there is a good chance you may not be eligible for a Colorado marijuana license.

In Washington not only are license applicants, financiers, and shareholders required to be criminally investigated, their spouses are subject to criminal record investigations and, to some degree, financial disclosure.

As a preliminary step it is a very good idea to determine if your spouse is or is not eligible for such a license. If there is something in his or her past which would disqualify him or her this needs to be brought to the attention of your lawyer at the earliest possible moment. There are often workarounds if full disclosure is made at an early stage in the process. However, if a background check discloses a disqualifying fact about your spouse you may very well, to use a term of art, be hooped.

As well as your spouse's potential downsides, what about his or her upsides? Is your spouse employed? Can you and your family live on his or her salary while you work on the marijuana business?

Finally, is your spouse supportive of your venture? Any business will have its ups and downs and it is important to know where your spouse or partner stands as you go into the business. If there are misgivings or hesitations it is vital that you listen to them. There is every chance your spouse has a pretty clear idea of your strengths and weaknesses. Pay attention.

1.4 Solvency

In most jurisdictions you have to provide full financial disclosure and grant the licensing authority the right to check on your tax and bank records. In many jurisdictions you will be required to account for the source of funds with which you plan to finance your marijuana business.

In different jurisdictions different records are required, but what the licensing authorities are looking for is a full financial portrait, warts and all. Are you prepared to provide everything from pay slips to deposit forms, details on your mortgage, credit card information, and other loans?

The major concern of the regulators tends to be making sure that the money going into the marijuana business is "clean." They do not want licensees to bring in criminally tainted funds. In the process, they also look to make sure you are up to date on your taxes, your child support payments, even things like parking tickets. The point is that a license is a privilege and not a right so regulators tend to be both intrusive and potentially sticky.

Many people have a clean — if sometimes messy and ill-recorded — financial life. Taking a look at your own finances, what is it going to take to put together the required disclosure for your license application? Do you have a personal accountant? If not, this may be the time to hire one.

1.5 Good credit?

Many jurisdictions will look at your credit rating and history as part of the vetting process during a license application. It is very much a judgment call and mild credit blemishes are unlikely to sink your application. On the other hand, a recent bankruptcy or a lot of overdue bills may raise red flags.

Beyond the licensing question, good credit may also be essential to either finance your marijuana business or to finance your life while you are trying to get the business up and running. It is not a bad idea to take a look at your personal balance sheet and consider your assets versus liabilities. Working with a good accountant, you may want to consider how you can create some personal liquidity prior to beginning the licensing process.

Wonderful as good credit is, actually getting a loan can be tough if you need the money "right now." It can be even tougher when you go from being employed to being in start-up mode. Worse, leaning across your banker's desk and asking for a loan for your marijuana business while you are, from the bank's perspective, unemployed is not a brilliant idea if it can be avoided with a little foresight and planning.

1.6 Reputation risks

In the US, marijuana is still illegal at the federal level. While the state law and federal forbearance make it unlikely you will be charged, the fact is you may be seen by some people as a criminal and by others as a drug pusher.

When you assess the marijuana retail opportunity it is important to take the potential for reputation damage into account. Some people are very deeply rooted in their community, their children's schools, their churches. Those roots may take a beating when you open your marijuana retail business.

It is often worthwhile to have a few preliminary conversations with friends, neighbors, pastors, and your kids' principal to gauge reaction. In a large urban environment, reputational risk can often be minimized simply because the connection between you and your marijuana business is not very obvious. However, in suburban and rural settings it may be very difficult not to be tagged as the owner of a dispensary or pot shop.

1.7 Professional risks

Lawyers, doctors, accountants, teachers, professors, and law enforcement personnel, to name but a few, may run professional risks if they are associated with the ownership and/or operation of a business operating contrary to criminal law.

The issues are complicated and depend on such things as the oaths which a person must take to become a lawyer or an accountant. They may also depend on certain legal obligations which professionals have in virtue of their profession. It makes good sense for any professional or quasi-professional to get in touch with his or her professional association prior to any ownership/ operating involvement of a marijuana business.

1.8 Support of friends and family

If you open a cupcake shop it is a good bet that your family and friends will cheer you on. They will come to the opening party, will probably buy your cupcakes and, when that nasty crunch comes and you need to borrow $10,000 to make it to the other side, they will help if they can. Can you count on that sort of support for your marijuana dispensary or pot shop?

Now is the time to think about that and, in many cases, to tell your friends and family what you hope to do. Don't be surprised if some people don't support your plans. It is better to know well in advance. At the same time, don't assume that you will have no support because it's pot. The fact is that a legal pot business, well run, is just as worthy of family and friends' support as a cupcake parlor. It is up to you to think about whether you will be proud of your business. Friends and family will make up their own minds.

2. Personality Traits

Going into business of any sort takes certain personality traits: independence, risk tolerance, grit. The retail marijuana business needs all these traits and more. The key thing to remember is that while a lot of things can be researched and learned, you are pretty much stuck with the personality you have. There is no point in making yourself miserable because you are not well-suited for independent business. Here are a few traits which are particularly important for the retail marijuana business.

2.1 Detail minded

Virtually every business requires a head for detail. Everything from ordering new stock to paying invoices to keeping track of employee hours means a lot of bookwork, which means hours sweating over a computer screen.

The regulated marijuana business is detail driven in a way other businesses are not. Regulators, in several jurisdictions, have adopted a "seed to sale" regulatory scheme in which every hundreth of a gram of cannabis has to be tracked from the point that the seed or, more often, clone, is put in the growing medium to the point where it is actually paid for and delivered to the customer. Along the way, the enormous amount of waste material which is part of the marijuana product cycle has to be tracked as well.

Additionally, if you are growing for sale or are purchasing from a wholesale grower (where legal in your jurisdiction) the strain of the marijuana as well as its relative potency (level of THC) may have to be tracked. If you are selling edibles you have to keep track of the total dose per package. Oils and concentrates have their own tracking demands.

This is in addition to the normal bookwork and inventory control any retail store involves. "Big picture" people can certainly hire people to track all this information and there are software systems designed specifically for the recordkeeping requirements of the marijuana industry but as the owner and the licensee, ultimately you are responsible for ensuring that your books and records can and will pass inspection, which means you have to be willing to drive down into the details.

2.2 Organized

While paying attention to the details is important, seeing how the details fit into the bigger picture of your business is critical. As the owner you have to be able to keep track of everything, from employee schedules to shipment dates, to when you are meeting with your accountant and the fact that you are running out of branded bags and that it is a four-week turnaround to get more.

Are you a person who makes lists? Whose smartphone controls your universe? Who doesn't even notice that he or she is multitasking? Who can stay in control even as waves of chaos crash against you? These are all attributes which are potentially valuable in any small business but all the more so in the marijuana space.

In a tightly regulated business, excellent organization can make the difference between compliance and potentially losing your license and investment. Keeping a clear desk, returning phone calls, answering email promptly, having a daily task list, and knowing the financial state of your business on a daily basis are all habits which will keep you compliant and thriving. But are they habits you have? There are plenty of people who are highly successful, deeply creative, and totally disorganized. If you are one of them you are not doing yourself any favors by getting into a tightly regulated, detail driven business.

2.3 Willing to co-operate with licensing and regulatory officials

What is your attitude towards authority? It is an odd question in a business book but crucial when it comes to a closely regulated business like marijuana. From the disclosures required in the licensing process, to ongoing inspection and accounting requirements for the operation of a marijuana dispensary or pot store in most jurisdictions, you are going into business with the government.

For some marijuana advocates the entire point of the legalization movement was a libertarian ideal of uncontrolled access to pot. That has not happened and the jurisdictions in which medical or recreational marijuana is legal have created intrusive, costly, regulatory regimes. These regimes, along with all manner of banking rules we'll deal with later, mean that the marijuana business is one of the most regulated retail businesses. Is this sort of governmental intrusion something with which you will be able to cooperate?

2.4 Addiction issues

Leave aside the science for a moment. There are some people who become psychologically addicted to marijuana. Yes, psychological addiction to marijuana is a real thing and it is something anyone going into the marijuana business needs to consider carefully. It is possible for an alcoholic to own and run a bar, but it is very difficult. Surrounded by temptation it is very easy to kick back and have more than a few drinks. Even high-functioning alcoholics can find themselves in real trouble running a bar.

If you have an addiction issue with marijuana it is probably a bad idea to open a pot shop or dispensary. Availability creates temptation and that can put your business and investment at considerable risk. It's something to think about, carefully.

3. Business Experience

Successful businesses tend to be run by people who have run successful businesses previously. However, many successful businesspeople have also had the experience of either owning or managing a business which failed. While success is a great thing, failure often teaches just as much.

When you are looking at going into the marijuana business it is important to sit down and make a list of your business experience. Such a list is usually part of the documentation required during the licensing process and it is a good way to consider whether you are in a place where you know enough and have enough experience to run a successful marijuana business.

A few questions to consider follow in the next sections.

3.1 Have you worked in retail?

Whether it is a marijuana dispensary or a pot shop, the legal marijuana business is all about retail: finding customers, having them visit your shop, selling them a product, taking their money, and making their visit to your store something they will want to do again. Keeping track of inventory, managing suppliers, dealing with point of sale computers and their interface to your inventory control, and a hundred other things all are part of running a retail operation.

Having hands-on retail experience is not an absolute prerequisite for success but it will certainly improve your chances. If you have retail experience, great. But what if you don't?

In most jurisdictions the licensing process takes several months. As you are waiting for your paperwork to be completed it might be a good idea to find a job or even an internship in a marijuana-related business or, if that is impossible, in a retail store. It does not take long to get the basics of retailing but plunging into your own new store without ever having rung up a sale should be avoided.

3.2 Have you ever run a business?

Have you ever been in charge of a business or even a part of a business where you made decisions about hiring and firing, ordering stock and supplies, and taking care of the hundreds of details which keep the business operating?

While you can get retail experience quickly and easily, the experience of running a business is both more valuable and more difficult to get on the fly. Once again, if you have run a business, great. But what if you haven't?

To a degree running a business is learned by running a business. However, there are many useful courses in small-business management, offered in community colleges and online. These are very basic but they walk you through issues such as leases, insurance, tax, human resources, elementary finance, and a number of other general business topics. As well, there are plenty of books on the subject such as *Start & Run a Retail Business*, also published by Self-Counsel Press. Do the courses, read the books.

If you have not run a business before you should also budget and plan to hire at least one person as a manager or consultant. This is likely to be expensive but worth it because not only will he or she get your business up and running, he or she will also teach you what you need to know about running your business.

3.3 Have you ever owned a business?

If you have run a business you will know that running a business and owning it are two very different things. When you run a business you are a manager and you have a set of responsibilities, but those responsibilities do not include making decisions about the conduct of that business. As a manager you steer the ship but you do not set the course.

As the owner of a business you decide on the strategy and then make decisions as to how to implement that strategy. If you have managers, they will give you information and often suggestions, but ultimately the strategic responsibility is yours, as is the responsibility to find financing, comply with the various laws and regulations surrounding your business, set a style for your business and, ultimately, make sure the business makes money.

People often combine owning a business with running that business and the two functions can appear pretty interchangeable, but the reality is that an owner has to have the capacity to step back and assess how his or her business is actually doing. If it is meeting its goals; if it is worth carrying on.

Ownership is particularly important in the regulated marijuana business, as in most jurisdictions, whether the business is incorporated or not, the licensing process is all about the owner. Changes in ownership must be approved in most cases and it is the owner who is personally liable for any infractions of the rules.

3.4 Have you ever had employees reporting to you?

Owning and running a one-person business is very different from owning and running a business with employees. Most marijuana businesses, whether medical or recreational, will have employees and you, as owner, will have to be prepared to operate in this environment. We'll discuss this in some detail later but consider what you know about —

🍁 advertising for employees,

- interviewing prospective employees,

- wages, salaries, and benefits,

- tax obligations respecting employees,

- basic onboarding paperwork,

- employment contracts including confidentiality,

- employee standards,

- employee training — initial and ongoing,

- vacations and sick days,

- employee manuals, and do you need one? (you do),

- unsatisfactory employee performance,

- written warnings and dismissal,

- wrongful dismissal, and

- discrimination, sexual harassment, and other pitfalls.

Most of an employer's relationship with his or her employees is about common sense and respect; however, prior to opening and operating a business you as the prospective owner of the business need to be aware of the responsibilities and legal obligations you are assuming when you hire employees.

4. Opportunity Cost

Opening a marijuana business means you will not be doing something else. This seems obvious but it is surprising how often an entrepreneur gets excited about a business opportunity without giving much thought to what else he or she could do or invest money in. It is also surprising how often entrepreneurs fail to consider an exit strategy. When you are doing a self-assessment, thinking about these issues is more than worthwhile.

4.1 What are you doing right now?

For a moment let's assume you are employed in a job you don't hate and are making $90,000 per year with a good healthcare plan. Let's assume you own a house worth $400,000 with a $200,000 mortgage. Your spouse also makes $90,000 a year and has health care. Let's further assume that you have a good credit rating, minimal credit card debt, and $50,000 in savings. You are solvent and gradually accumulating wealth and, perhaps, a pension entitlement. You are 40.

If you decide to become a marijuana entrepreneur, a number of things are going to change. You will give up your job and your healthcare coverage, you will invest all or most of your savings, you may take a second mortgage, and you are likely to stress your credit. Your family net income will be cut in half and your mortgage will increase.

By going into business you are betting that you can, at minimum, replace your foregone income and savings and repay any second mortgage you take to finance the business. That is the breakeven position. The fact is that you are assuming risk as well as making an investment, and that risk needs to be offset with a better than breakeven return.

When you come to doing the financial spreadsheets for your business plan, it is important to bear in mind that risk without significant return is a losing proposition. Consider what sort of return you actually require for the risks you are taking. Then look at the projections and see if that return is going to be available and, as important, how soon.

Businesses look at Return on Investment (ROI) as a metric for success. It is certainly important. However, ROI does not factor in what a business owner gives up in order to start and run a business. If you invest $100,000 in your business and have a net ROI of 20 percent you are only seeing $20,000 a year. Much better than you would get from a savings account, but unless you are also drawing a salary, that ROI does not replace much lost income.

4.2 What is your time horizon?

Do you see yourself working in the marijuana business for the rest of your career or is this more of an excursion into a business which may offer significant returns? If it is an excursion, how long is the tour?

Business planning exercises always have a time dimension. Daily sales lead to monthly, quarterly, and then yearly. With startups there are usually months and even years where the business has a negative cash flow. That is, you spend more money than you make and that negative cash flow has to be covered. Making a loss for a couple of years is not uncommon in typical retail businesses and understanding that from the beginning will help you plan your business. The question is how long would you be prepared to stick with a loss-making or breakeven business and why?

On the upside, there is no reason to believe that your marijuana business will not be a roaring success from day one. If you have done your planning, scoped out your market, got a real handle on your cost of goods sold, kept other costs minimal, and have lots of inexpensive financing, you might be sitting on a green gold mine.

4.2a What is your ideal position five years down the road?

Five years is an arbitrary number but it pretty much captures the mid-term. Do you want to be a successful marijuana entrepreneur with a bustling retail store (or two or three)? How much of an owner's draw would you need? Do you want to buy out or repay your investors?

Would you like to be someone who did well out of the marijuana business but has moved on? In this case would you want to sell your business outright or would you be more interested in becoming a silent partner and enjoying the income from an ongoing business operated either by an active partner or a management team?

It may seem premature to ask these questions before you have even begun drafting a business plan or structured the licensed entity, but these are key questions because how you answer them will affect things like corporate structure, what level of return you need to see in your projections, the arrangements you make with your investors, and a host of other business details. Being able to tell your lawyer and your accountant what your end game is allows them to do their jobs much more effectively.

4.3 Personal exit strategy

When you are in the thick of starting up and then running your marijuana business you are not going to have a lot of time to consider how and even if you will exit the business you are working so hard to set up. This is why thinking about your exit as a matter of business preliminaries is important.

One of the advantages of incorporation — where it is available under the marijuana regulations in your jurisdiction — is that it is a relatively straightforward business to sell all or some of the shares in the company down the road. Now there will be the issue of a change of control affecting the license; but that is an issue regardless of business structure chosen.

Your lawyer will advise you about other considerations which affect a personal exit strategy. Things like partnership or shareholders agreements, personal guarantees for debt financing, and the obligations of a director to his shareholders all raise potential issues; issues which are a great deal easier to resolve at the beginning of a business than four or five years into it.

Any business planning exercise needs to consider the exit strategy of the principal or principals of the business. While you may set a value goal — "When the business is worth 1 million dollars" — realize that value can be difficult even in a successful business. (I will go into this in more detail later in the book.)

Taking time to self-assess at the outset will save you a great deal of time down the road. It will also give you a good idea of your own strengths and weaknesses. Armed with your own self-assessment you are in a good position to move on to a preliminary assessment of your potential involvement in the marijuana business.

Preliminary Business Matters

2

Self assessment in hand, it is time to draw together the information and people you need to create a business plan, which we will discuss in Chapter 3. For now, having identified your strengths and weaknesses, as well as your experience, think about how best you can structure a marijuana business for success.

Because of the licensing requirements in the legal marijuana business, some key decisions need to be considered prior to actually setting out a business plan. Because of some of the wrinkles in the regulatory scheme in your jurisdiction, the conventional sequence of creating a business plan, coming up with financing, and then working on operations may not be possible or may have to be very carefully considered.

This is the stage in the planning process where all your options are open and research can really pay off. Digging deep online is easy and rewarding (but always remember that online sources may be unreliable).

The marijuana business has its roots in activism and there are an amazing number of resources available online and off: forums, business associations, and marijuana specialist professionals all can add to your information. Talking to suppliers, potential landlords, people already in the marijuana business and, where possible, regulators can give you great information, and save you time and a lot of money.

If you are in a jurisdiction where medical or recreational marijuana is already legal, you need to spend some time visiting stores already in business. Yes, you may become a competitor but, right now, you are simply a businessperson looking at opportunities.

1. Professional Advice

Every business needs professional advice. Having an accountant and a lawyer who work with you from the beginning is an investment which will pay off because your business will be structured optimally to meet your purposes.

In a regulated business like legal marijuana, having a lawyer and accountant is an absolute necessity. Finding and managing professionals is not obvious but it is often a matter of knowing what you need before you begin.

In general, here are a few pointers when hiring professionals:

- Ideally they have done this work before.
- If not, they should be familiar with licensed businesses.
- They should be familiar with small businesses.
- They should be familiar with start-ups.
- They should have good references which you can check.
- They should offer realistic quotes.
- You should take your time to ensure you make the right decision.

It is important when you are interviewing professionals to make it clear that you plan to open a dispensary or pot shop. Professionals need to know the exact nature of the business they will be advising. If a professional is uncomfortable with your business for moral or legal reasons it is best to move on to someone who accepts your business.

Even better than acceptance is experience. In most states where medical or recreational marijuana has been legalized there are lawyers who specialize in the field. Google will give the names and a good deal of information about lawyers who know the ins and outs of your local regulations.

The lawyer's role in advising you on the law and regulations in your jurisdiction is critical; however, in terms of setting up your business an accountant who knows the marijuana business may be even more important.

Part of the regulatory scheme in most jurisdictions is a very careful accounting of marijuana products. Accountants don't just deal with money, and some are very good at designing systems which allow easy tracking.

There are also plenty of rules which cover where you get the money to start your marijuana business and the requirement that this money be "clean." A good accountant can be invaluable when it comes to tracking funds.

Setting up a company's books is not complicated for most businesses. However, in the United States, in the medical marijuana business the impact of tax laws is complicated by the fact what the business is selling is illegal under current federal law. That may mean that a marijuana business is liable to be taxed on its gross income without standard business deductions because those deductions are not available to that business. This is potentially a huge problem and one which may require some sophisticated accounting and legal solutions.

Finding, interviewing, and retaining excellent professional advisors at the earliest stages of your drive towards opening your business will ensure that you start with solid foundations.

2. Consultants

In the midst of the Green Rush, many people have set up as consultants with respect to virtually every aspect of the marijuana business. There are highly trained plant specialists who teach the art of cloning particular varieties; there are people who know, or purport to know, how to set up a medical marijuana dispensary or a successful recreational shop. There are systems consultants and compliance specialists as well.

Consultants can offer significant shortcuts in the road to getting your marijuana business up and running. They charge fees for doing this and, sometimes, will look for an equity position as well. It is very much a judgment call as to whether to bring on one or many consultants. If you decide to go the consultant route you have to be very careful as to who you contract. Basic due diligence — references, completed projects, fees, contract terms, and conditions — all needs to be done.

If you are going to bring on a consultant you need to be clear about what you want that consultant to actually achieve and at what cost. If you want a point-of-sale to inventory computer solution, a consultant may be the best way to go simply because the scope of the work is defined and constrained.

3. Banking

In a normal business one of the things people routinely do is set up a business bank account.

At this moment in the marijuana business, particularly in the US, banking — from having a business checking account to obtaining loans to allowing credit and debit card payments — for the marijuana industry is extremely difficult. Once again, the problem is that the sale of marijuana is illegal at the federal level. Despite federal banking regulators indicating that they have no wish to prosecute bankers who extend facilities to marijuana businesses, the fact is that individual bankers are very uncomfortable with marijuana businesses as bank clients.

Recent advice from federal banking regulators in the US was supposed to help in that it made the bankers' obligations more clear. However, by imposing a duty to have positive knowledge that the funds from a marijuana operation were legally obtained, the government guidance has actually made it, in many cases, more difficult for marijuana retail operations to obtain banking services. Solutions are emerging but banking remains a huge problem for marijuana retail operations in many US jurisdictions.

Here is where the advice of an accountant familiar with the marijuana industry is invaluable. First off, not all banks are gun shy. Second, part of the reluctance of a given bank may rest on the perception that people in the marijuana business are simply untrustworthy: Having an accountant to certify your books and records can go some distance towards building trust. Finally, where you cannot get a bank, an accountant is often able to set up structures which will allow you to run your business as a cash operation while still staying within the law and having the records necessary for tax purposes.

4. Marijuana Licensing: Walk-through

Once you have a lawyer, but before drafting your business plan, it's a good idea to walk through the licensing requirements for your jurisdiction as well as the eligibility rules.

The first step is to familiarize yourself with the types of licenses available in your jurisdiction. Each jurisdiction varies but there are two main types of retail marijuana license: medical and recreational. In each jurisdiction the operational rules for each type tend to differ. For example, medical marijuana licenses tend to require a seed-to-sale control over the product. Recreational licenses usually allow the licensee to purchase the product from a wholesaler or licensed grower. Medical licenses only allow sales to people who are certified medical users under that jurisdiction's regulations; recreational licenses let you sell to everybody over a certain age. As well, the type of license you have will tend to determine the amount of tax you pay or must charge in your jurisdiction.

The type of license you apply for will have enormous impacts on the business model you can use for your business. However, whether you apply for a medical or a recreational (where available) license, you will still have to meet strict eligibility requirements. Having a conversation with your lawyer about the type of license you want and the materials required to be filed early on in the process will save you money and time.

A lawyer who has made license applications before will have a familiarity with the sorts of material which may attract unwanted regulatory attention. You will be putting together most of the material yourself, but having your lawyer review the material before you submit it will let the lawyer "red flag" problematic material and deal with it promptly and effectively.

For example, the sudden deposit of $126,000 in your savings account is potentially problematic in states which require the submission of bank records. It can also trigger anti-money-laundering notifications in both Canada and the US. However, if your application contains a note that that sum was your share of your Uncle Hank's estate and a bit of supporting material is included in the application, the problem will be solved before it arises.

In some cases lawyers specializing in a particular area will have established relationships with the regulators. At the preliminary stages this gives them the ability to make a call or write a letter on behalf of an unnamed client with a particular problem. While this does not make the problem go away, the regulator will often tell the lawyer, in general, what the regulator wants to see or not see.

5. Incorporation

There are many reasons to create a company to operate your marijuana business. Before you incur the expense of incorporation, it is important to determine if an incorporated entity can hold the sort of license you are seeking in your jurisdiction. In some jurisdictions there is a requirement that a medical marijuana dispensary be set up on a cooperative or nonprofit basis rather than as a for-profit company.

The decision to incorporate is affected by many factors. This is particularly true where you are operating a heavily regulated business which, at the moment, suffers from banking and tax disabilities and penalties at a federal level. Professional advisors may suggest corporate structures which can minimize the impact of these disabilities and penalties. For example, isolating the marijuana operations in a separate licensed company while keeping the remainder of the operations in another company may create significant tax advantages, in that the non-marijuana company would be allowed such things as typical business deductions which the marijuana company would not. This sort of structure is how accountants and lawyers earn their fees and improve your business's chances of success. The IRS has recently provided guidance which has destroyed the viability of many such schemes. The rules can change and you need a lawyer and an accountant who keep up with the changes.

Other reasons to incorporate include the reduction of personal liability, the ability to attract and structure financing, and the capacity to have your marijuana business operate at arm's length from your other business and personal interests. However, it is important to understand that virtually every jurisdiction's regulatory scheme requires extensive information about the directors, officers, and shareholders of any corporation seeking a license for the marijuana business even where there is a company in place.

6. Rules on Ownership and Management

Most jurisdictions have licensing and operating rules going to ownership of a marijuana business. These rules are imposed at the license application stage and whenever a change in ownership occurs.

As a matter of business preliminaries, you need to consider who will own the business and, with the help of your lawyer, determine what "ownership" means under the rules in your jurisdiction. Important considerations include how the marijuana business is structured; if it is incorporated, who owns the shares; if a limited partnership, who the partners are. Who finances the business, regardless of ownership stake, is something that concerns licensing authorities. Finally, regardless of who owns the business, the regulator is concerned with who is the governing person of that business and/or who is the "true party of interest." (Washington, Colorado, and other states have similar regulatory intent.)

The intent is to ensure that licenses are only granted to people who are eligible under the rules. Because holding a license is a privilege and not a right, the regulators, providing they act in a procedurally fair way, are entitled to be very strict when it comes to ownership, management, and financing.

7. A Clean Application

Working with your lawyer and accountant, and prior to writing up your business plan, it is important to walk through every element of the application for a marijuana license in your jurisdiction.

Even where there is nothing which is in any way dubious, spending the time to organize the application and gather together the supporting materials and required information will improve your chances of approval.

Where there is an element which might raise questions, identifying and dealing with it at the earliest stage will give you options going forward.

The regulator is looking for a clean application which raises no red flags, is complete, and is responsive to the concerns which the regulator in each jurisdiction has usually made very clear.

8. Capital

How much it will cost to open your marijuana business will be dealt with in detail at the business plan stage. Coming up with a preliminary budget and then looking at your funding options makes sense at an early stage.

8.1 How much will you need?

How much do you need up front? Here is a partial list of basic costs; you'll want to get hard numbers attached to each of these in the business planning exercise but this will get you started:

- Premises
- Fixtures
- Licenses
- Stock
- Packaging
- Employees
- Security
- Insurance
- Utilities
- Taxes
- Professional fees
- Advertising and marketing

This list is for a retail operation which is not growing its own product or processing raw product into oils or edibles. Some of these costs will have to be paid up front even before you get your license, some will have to be paid before you can open your doors, and some will be ongoing regardless of what, if any, revenue you bring in.

Your accountant can be incredibly useful in coming up with approximate numbers for these costs and also help you make educated guesses as to how long you will have to pay these costs from the business's capital account before revenue begins to cover them.

If you look at the list above you will see some items which are simply fixed costs. For example, there is likely a standard fee for a license application in your jurisdiction. Try to attach hard numbers where possible. There are other items such as "premises" where there can be a wide variation depending on things like the size of the space you think you need, location, and the commercial real estate market in your city or town.

Making a few calls to real estate agents and store supply businesses will let you get a range of prices. Keep track of those calls because, when you get your license, you will want to get in touch with these agents and suppliers.

When it comes to things like stock, packaging, advertising, and marketing, you are going to have to estimate. Those estimates will form the basis of your pro forma accounts and you want them to be as accurate as possible.

The Art of Estimating

A business is all about interconnected parts: If you add to your advertising spend, you anticipate that your sales will increase which means you have to have more stock on hand and more employees to serve the customers who come in as a result of the advertising. Every variable is, to some degree, connected to every other variable.

When you are attempting to estimate it is critical to hold at least one variable constant while you see what effect changes have on the other variables. For a retail store, a realistic constant is daily gross sales per customer.

In simplest terms, if you think you will sell an average of $30 per customer you can calculate the effect on your business of varying levels of traffic. Twenty customers a day is $600, 100 a day is $3,000. If medical or recreational marijuana is already legal in your jurisdiction take a look at your competition's pricing.

From that single constant you can work backward to calculate reasonable estimates for the costs associated with servicing that customer. These are back of the envelope calculations, but they will let you come up with plausible estimates of sales, cost of product, employees, security costs, required size and location of premises, and therefore the cost of renting or leasing those premises.

🌿 🌿 🌿

You can improve the accuracy of your estimates by doing a bit of legwork. If there are medical or recreational marijuana businesses in your city or nearby, spend a few hours scouting them. Actually count how many people go in the door. When are they busy? How busy are they?

Want revenue estimates? Google is your friend. A quick search revealed that Seattle, Washington's first recreational pot store, Uncle Ike's, made nearly $17,000 on launch day and then dropped back to $13,700 a day for the rest of the week. Your situation will be different, but by looking at various reports on the Internet, some information released by tax and regulatory authorities, and online discussions you can reach a realistic estimate.

Now there are some big factors: What is the regulatory burden of your license? For example, in Colorado, if you open a medical marijuana dispensary, you are required to grow your own marijuana with all the issues in terms of space, costs, waste, and tracking that implies. (The Colorado recreational market has been allowed to buy from wholesalers since 2014.)

That regulatory burden goes to your startup costs, but it also goes to Cost of Goods Sold (COGS). COGS will determine what is left over when you sell a quantity of marijuana for a set price. In a simple COGS model, the goods come from a wholesaler and you pay a price per pound or kilogram. You then split that into smaller units and sell it. The simple model has a pound being purchased at, say, $1,000 and then split into ounces which sell for $200, your gross margin would be $2,200.

In your business plan, you are going to get fairly granular on the expenses which will come off this gross margin, however, if you are in the United States, you need to pay attention to one huge elephant in the room: Section 280E of the Internal Revenue Code:

> No deduction or credit shall be allowed for any amount paid or incurred during the taxable year in carrying on any trade or business if such trade or business (or the activities which comprise such trade or business) consists of trafficking in controlled substances (within the meaning of schedule I and II of the Controlled Substances Act) which is prohibited by federal law or the law of any state in which such trade or business is conducted.

This section of the Internal Revenue Code means that a medical or recreational marijuana business will be taxed on the basis of its gross margin and that none of the standard business deductions are permitted. The effect of this tax rule goes right to the bottom line where marijuana retailers can see an effective tax burden of 40–70 percent and some have reported losing 90 percent of their gross to the government.

Creative lawyers and accountants have managed to reduce this burden somewhat by seeking to place many marijuana retail business operations outside the strict definition of "trafficking" but the IRS countered with a memo in January, 2015, significantly narrowing the sorts of deductions permitted. Consult your lawyer and accountant as early as possible in the process to minimize your own marijuana business's exposure.

Think about employees and how much a good bud tender (a.k.a., retail clerk) will cost per hour. Will you need a manager? What about security?

Get some basic business insurance quotes and make sure to mention that you are going to be in the marijuana business. A quote for a pet food store will likely be a lot lower than one for a marijuana retail operation.

Ask your professional advisors for estimates on their fees to license and for ongoing services.

Take a look at the advertising your competition is doing. Where do they advertise? Do they have websites? Are they in online directories and store locating apps? What do those things cost?

Think about state and local taxes. In Colorado, state medical marijuana attracts a 2.9 percent sales tax plus local taxes; recreational pot is subject to the 2.9 percent sales tax plus a 10 percent state marijuana sales tax plus local taxes. Local taxes vary by city and district. These taxes are passed through to your customers, but you need cash at the end of the month to cover them.

Finally, take the high end of your estimates for each of these items, add them up and add a 15–20 percent contingency factor.

This rough budget will give you the ability to think seriously about what it will take to open your marijuana business. It will also give you some numbers to work with on a goal setting and "what if" basis.

For example: If you are planning on growing as well as selling retail in either a medical or a recreational context, you can think about whether it makes sense to have a grow-op feed a single retail outlet or if there is an argument for having more than one outlet tied to the grow-op or, where permitted, would it make sense to build out a grow-op to supply your retail operations plus have production left over for wholesale? Look at all the options and what those options imply in terms of capitalization.

There is no right answer. However there are constraints. Check your local jurisdiction's rules as to the size of the shop or dispensary — are there state, provincial, or municipal rules? Check marijuana supply: Are you allowed to buy wholesale? From whom? Do they have marijuana ready to go when you get your license?

Think about your own business model. A clinic selling medicine? A pot shop selling inexpensive pot to the masses? An artisanal, microbrew approach where prices are higher but varietals; natural, organic, production methods; and devotion to the higher end of cannabis culture drives the business model? Each of these models and dozens of others can be successful, but you have to decide which model is the best fit for you.

Finally, how much money you need is, to a degree, about what sort of return is likely to be generated on that money: A small amount promising a high return but at the cost of significant risk or a larger amount yielding a smaller return but with a lower risk? How much money you need is constrained at the bottom end by the minimal compliance requirements of the jurisdiction you are in; there really is no upper limit.

8.2 How much do you have?

There may be no effective upper limit to how much you can spend licensing, opening, and operating a marijuana business, but there is a limit to how much money you have to put into the business.

The retail marijuana business is unlike many in that it cannot, presently, be financed at banks, at least not directly. So what are your sources of funds?

8.2a Personal

Be creative. What have you got in your savings account? That's a start. Now look at things like investments, retirement savings, equity in your house (second mortgage?), your spouse's income, his or her savings, and your credit rating and credit cards. All in, how much can you raise?

8.2b Friends and family

If you are lucky enough to have wealthy parents who are willing to support your marijuana business don't be shy, ask for the money. Make sure that you have your lawyer and accountant deal with the details. If your parents flat out give you the money that is one thing, but if it is a loan then they will likely be seen as "financiers" for purposes of the licensing system which will lead to such things as criminal record checks and fingerprinting. The same is true for siblings and even rich old Aunt Myrna. Don't be surprised if a licensing body takes a dim view of ten $15,000 "gifts" two weeks before you apply for a license.

There is a wise old saying that family money is the most expensive money a new business can have. Depends on the family of course, but make sure you are very clear with your parents, siblings, and brother-in-law, that there are very real risks in the marijuana business.

Friends can be a source of funds but they are likely to be treated as financiers or investors for regulatory purposes and it is simpler to create a structure which allows them to invest according to the rules of your jurisdiction.

8.2c Investors

The general class of investors covers everyone who is not directly related to you (and some who are). Often, investors are people you have been in business with before and who think you are smart/can make them money. They can be people you work with, or complete strangers you find through brokers or lawyers or accountants or at your yoga class. (I am not going to go into such things as public offerings here.) As well, there are some institutional investors who are looking for opportunities in the marijuana space, as are some angel investors.

Investment can come in many forms ranging from partnerships, shares in limited companies, units in limited partnerships, term loans, and royalty agreements. Raising money from investors can be quite informal or very formal indeed with contracts, guarantees, security agreements, and all manner of other, often expensive, legal paraphernalia.

Virtually every arm's length investor in a start-up will try to minimize the amount of money invested, maximize the share of the business he or she gets for the investment, and get as much security as possible against the loss of those investments. Be prepared to negotiate.

8.3 A number

Once you have added up your own money, family and friends' money, and investor money you will have a number. Well, actually, a range of numbers. The fact is that the only sure money for your business is the money you personally have. Every other bit of money depends on other people deciding to and coming through with investing in your business.

Making your own number as large as possible gives you a starting point. If you take that number, and ignore other sources of investment, you can compare it to the capital requirements you have worked out earlier. This can be a sobering moment if your resources are not sufficient to cover your projected start-up costs; but it is also a moment where the reality of your projected business begins to take shape. Can you trim your start-up number? Can you find more personal funds? Can you gain commitments from friends, family, and investors?

As you move forward in the business planning process, having a real sense of what you can afford to invest and what you can reasonably expect others to invest keeps the entire process real. While friends and family may be willing to "take a flyer" on your marijuana business, investors will want to know how you will pay them back their money and pay the return on investment they expect.

9. Resources

Throughout the process of self-assessment and preliminary business planning you are going to be doing a lot of research. You will be talking to lawyers, accountants, consultants, potential competitors, suppliers, commercial real estate agents, designers, growers, and a host of other people. You will also be online, learning about the nature of the marijuana business.

As you move from preliminary business planning to actually writing up a business plan and then executing that plan, the contacts you have made are going to be very valuable, if you can find them. All too often a name and a number or an email address is scrawled on a piece of paper which is immediately lost. Great online articles are forgotten.

From the get-go you need to keep your resources organized.

Some people are so clever with their smartphones that they are able to put together an entire project with nothing more than Evernote and a folder full of bookmarks. For the rest of us, investing $10 in a hardbound, lined notebook can be a lifesaver. As you accumulate material and names and business cards, make dated notes. Keep your to-do lists in the notebook. Write your appointments and notes on phone calls in the book. Tape the business cards you pick up onto the pages. In a few weeks the book will look awful but you will have the information you need at your fingertips.

Once a week take your phone and snap a picture of each page of your notebook. Now you have it backed up and available on your phone.

When you open the doors of your marijuana business that notebook — and it will likely have expanded to a few notebooks — will hold every bit of information you have acquired. Keep it updated as you run your business. Your circle of contacts and connections will grow and you will have every name, number, and email where it can be found.

A simple Google search for, say, recreational marijuana in "x" will give you more information than you can use. The key thing to remember is that online information is a starting point. It is of mixed quality and some of it is simply wrong. But using online resources to inform yourself before speaking with lawyers or consultants is important. Reading online sources ranging from marijuana business forums to LinkedIn, which has several excellent marijuana business groups, to Quora.com, where there are many questions about the marijuana business posted and some excellent answers, is the homework which will improve your chances of success.

In jurisdictions where medical or recreational marijuana is legal there are various associations of store and dispensary owners which can provide information. In jurisdictions where cannabis is not yet legal, there are advocacy groups pushing for legalization. Getting involved with these associations can provide you with solid information about the state of the marijuana business in your jurisdiction.

Writing a Business Plan

3

When you have completed your own self-assessment, researched the marijuana regulatory system in your jurisdiction, done the preliminary business analysis and revenue and expense calculations, and, ideally, have your professional advisors in place, you are ready to write a business plan for your marijuana business.

Before you do, it is worth thinking about what business plans are actually for: Who is the intended audience? Every business plan has at least two audiences: an internal audience which may consist of no one but yourself, and the external audience(s) which may include investors, potential partners, the regulator, stakeholders ranging from potential employees to people in the neighborhood and, possibly, potential buyers for your business down the road.

Every one of these audiences wants to understand some basics about your proposed business: What are you going to do? How are you going to do it? How much money will you need? Where is that money coming from and how will it be spent? What revenue do you anticipate? What expenses? What milestones do you expect to reach? When?

1. Your Business Plan Is a Marketing Piece

People often think of business plans as exercises in accounting and guesswork, which they are, to a degree.

However, a business plan is best understood as the marketing which you are doing for your vision of a business.

The facts and figures have to be right because they are all about your credibility as a businessperson. Those facts and figures are not, however, all there is in the business plan. They are the base on which you make your business case and your business case needs to reflect more than just a healthy return on investment; it has to reflect your personal commitment to the business.

Yes, your business plan is going to be read by savvy, cynical people. They will be looking for inconsistencies and will try and poke holes in your assumptions, but they will also be looking for your passion and conviction that your business is going to work.

When investors or potential partners or financiers look at a business plan they want the numbers to make sense, but what they are even more concerned about is that you, as the owner and operator, understand the numbers and how they relate to the operations of the business. Great numbers are really only a part of a business plan: the rest is the conviction of the founder that this idea, this particular retail marijuana business makes sense.

So, as you read through this chapter think about how you can convince first yourself and then investors, potential partners, regulators, and even your spouse that your business plan really is going to work.

2. It's Your Business Plan

We'll walk through a template below but, before we do, let's consider what you will get out of the exercise.

When you began you had a business idea: Open a marijuana-based retail store. If you have done the work suggested in the previous chapters you now have a pretty good idea of what that actually means given the reality of the regulations in your jurisdiction and the basic economics of marijuana. You will have become familiar with the basic idea of return on investment, cost of goods sold, and gross and net revenue.

The first decision you have to make writing your business plan is what your own motive is for going into the marijuana business. Do you see the marijuana business as a potentially very profitable business or would you be content with low profits or even no profits in order to participate in cannabis culture? Is your marijuana business intended as an investment along with other investments or will it be an owner operated, stand-alone business and the main focus of your attention?

These are foundational questions which only you can answer. But they are important to ask because the answers to these questions will set the course for your business and therefore your business plan.

The second decision you need to make is about the level of detail you need or want to include in your business plan and how to present that detail. This is very much a balancing act. Too much detail and you will lose your audience and spend too much time building the business plan; too little and some audiences (particularly potential investors or partners) will be left with unanswered questions and may move on.

A wise old accountant friend of mine pointed out that business, particularly retail business, is actually very simple: You buy something for a dollar and sell it for two dollars, everything else is accounting. When you are writing a business plan, at minimum, you need to explain where and for how much you will obtain the goods you are selling and you need to show how you will be able to sell those goods at the price you require to cover expenses and create a return on investment. Which means, at the heart of your business plan will be some very basic accounting and some projections.

The third decision you need to make is what the useful time frame for your business plan actually is. Your business will exist across time. The further into the future you project the less certain your numbers are going to be.

The reason you need to decide on the time frame before actually drafting the business plan is that once a business plan is written there is a tendency for external audiences to measure your business's performance against the estimates it contains. This is not a terribly reasonable tendency but it is very real and you, as a business owner, need to take it into account.

You also need to take into account the actual life cycle of a business. Every business exists for a period before it opens its doors and makes its first sale. Again, the idea of a start-up phase is well understood in business and the fact you will be spending money for months or even years before you make your first sale needs to be included in your plan, and you need to explain where you are going to get the money to finance this phase.

At the other end of the cycle, when your business is up and running, you need to think about how far into the future you want to run your projections and what assumptions you will be making. Putting in projected monthly revenues and expenses for, say, the first two years of operations may make a lot of sense, but extending those monthly projections out to five years or even ten, while easy to do on a spreadsheet, is unlikely to add much useful or reliable information for your reader.

Finally, you have to decide on the milestones you want to reach and when you can reach them. Using a milestone rather than a goal-driven approach creates a measurable, finite series of stages for your business to go through. It is a useful distinction: A milestone is a measure of actual performance. "Three months after I began, I finished the first draft of my book" is different from saying "I will finish my book by the end of May, 2016."

If you decide to write your business plan with milestones to be reached by specific dates, you make your business and yourself accountable. Either you are open for business on November 1, 2017 or you are not. If you are, you have done what you said you were going to do. If not, you have missed that milestone and need to work harder and smarter to reach the next one.

A good business plan, even if you as the business owner are its only reader, outlines the positive conditions for the success of your business. Implicit in those conditions of success are the measurements of potential failure. Having a realistic, data-driven approach to the milestones of success will also give you an early warning system for potential failure.

3. Business Plan Content

If you pop over to Wikipedia — a great place to start your research — you'll find this list of the typical contents of a business plan for a start-up venture:

1. Cover page and table of contents
2. Executive summary
3. Mission statement
4. Business description
5. Business and regulatory environment analysis
6. SWOT analysis
7. Industry background
8. Operations plan
9. Competitor analysis
10. Market analysis
11. Marketing plan
12. Management summary
13. Financial plan
14. Attachments and milestones
15. Exit strategy

As an outline this will serve as well as any (and it is available in the download kit as a template for you to work from). However, look at what is missing from the perspective of a retail marijuana business: license requirements, regulatory environment, and security. Plus, while a financial plan may include these, you will want what are known as pro forma profit and loss statements as well as revenue and expense projections in the financial plan section. Finally, you need to include an exit strategy.

Let's walk through.

3.1 Cover page and table of contents

A cover page is important if your business plan is going to be out in the world. If it is going to be on an investor's desk it will be competing with other business plans, so think seriously about design. You are going into the retail business and your success is going to depend on intangibles such as branding, product differentiation, and look and feel. Understanding this from the get-go, and showing you understand it by having a slick, well-designed cover for your business plan will make that all-important great first impression.

Your cover page also gives you the opportunity to prove you can step beyond the graphic and design clichés of the marijuana business. There is no rule that every dispensary has to display a green marijuana leaf. Investing some time and a bit of money to work with a gifted designer will help your business plan and the rest of the graphic presentation of your business.

The table of contents is less problematic but needs thought. What level of granularity does your reader need? Headings, subheadings? Sure. But try to make them interesting. This is your first opportunity to impress a potential investor or partner and their first opportunity to say, "Not interested." Don't let them say that.

3.2 Executive summary

Business wisdom says that you write the executive summary after you have written the business plan, which makes some sense, since it is a summary of the rest of the plan; however, writing a draft executive summary can focus your thoughts and give you some direction in writing the rest of the plan.

A good executive summary is short. One page is good. An executive summary is first and foremost a marketing piece. You want to get your readers' attention and make them want to read on. The table of contents has already told your reader what is in the business plan; the executive summary should tell them why they should care and, when the plan is going to potential investors or partners, it needs to make the business case up front.

A "business case" is a fancy name for the argument in favor of your vision of your marijuana business. A sentence as simple as "The legalization of recreational marijuana in X has created the opportunity to make significant returns from a well-run cannabis store" will tell the prospective investor what you intend to prove in the rest of the plan.

A statement such as, "In year one we project gross sales of $500,000 and a 9 percent net margin" alerts the investor to your financial assumptions.

Writing concrete, measurable statements in the executive summary tells the reader that you are presenting a well-thought-out plan. While you may want to grab attention with a sentence like, "Recreational marijuana in the state of X is estimated to be a $2.5 billion a year industry," the fact is that your business plan is about a store in a particular location selling to a particular market. Getting those details in the executive summary will improve your credibility.

Most investors or potential partners will flip right to the executive summary and, unless it impresses them, they will not read most of the rest of your material as it is presented. They might skip to your financials and then, maybe, look at some of your other sections if you are lucky. The executive summary is your best shot at making your case.

Give your reader some real meat right up front. A paragraph stating, "XYZ Co. has retained the services of Jo Brown, Attorney, and Sam Green, Accountant who have assisted in the preparation of this business plan" gives the reader two names to Google. If Jo is a recognized marijuana business lawyer and Sam shows up in a search as a marijuana-business savvy accountant, your credibility will increase before your reader has even looked at the rest of the plan. "We have entered into a nondisclosure agreement with ABC Edibles to test their Mountain High cannabis infused granola" is another meaty sentence which gives your reader a hard point of reference.

A good executive summary is a teaser which will make your reader want to find out more, since it goes up front and is usually read first. The more hard information you include the more enticing your project will seem.

3.3 Mission statement

A mission statement is a short statement such as "To sell high quality marijuana at fair prices." Think about whether yours is one which your potential investors, partners, regulators, employees, customers, stakeholders, and neighbors will all endorse. An investor traditionally wants high prices rather than fair prices. "High quality marijuana" is often a matter of taste.

The problem with mission statements is that, while companies often feel they need them, they are sometimes vague, meaningless, or startlingly irrelevant. Worse, coming up with a mission statement can be a distracting waste of time at a stage in a business's development where time is very precious.

Unless you already have one, leave the page blank and see what develops in the course of writing the rest of your business plan.

3.4 Business description

Unlike a mission statement, a business description is grounded in the practical reality of what you are planning to actually do.

It need not be long but should be comprehensive. For a medical marijuana dispensary you would want to include things like information about the practical benefits of marijuana. For a pot shop you might want to include a description of the style or look and feel of the shop. For either, you would want to indicate where the business will be located and that you plan to be in full compliance with the regulations governing this type of business.

3.5 Business and regulatory environment analysis

Marijuana, whether recreational or medical, is a relatively new sort of business. It is also a heavily regulated business. Your reader needs to understand what external factors affect the business you are planning to start.

The business environment is just that: everything from the rental price of retail space in the area in which you are interested, to the availability of employees, to things like advertising and marketing requirements. Some of this analysis will be applicable to any business, some will be very specific to the marijuana industry and the business you are planning.

The regulatory analysis needs to provide a short history of the marijuana laws in your jurisdiction, a summary of the licensing requirements, an indication of where you are in the licensing process, and what business effects the rules in your jurisdiction will have. (You may wish to have a separate section for regulatory issues.)

As well, the issues of the non-deductibility of normal-course business expenses and the difficulties marijuana businesses have with banking, credit cards, loans, and transfers need to be discussed here.

Generally, the information presented in this analysis section should be factual. If there are problems your marijuana business will face, it is better to lay them out in the course of your fact-driven analysis without comment. However, it is often useful to include a reference to the sections of the business plan where these challenges are addressed.

As well as analyzing the business and regulatory environment, this is an excellent place to discuss the particular niche you see your marijuana business as filling. You'll be doing competitive analysis later; for the moment, where is the opportunity for your business? What needs do potential customers have which are not currently being met?

When you think about business environment, remember that retail is local. A retail business's success can be affected by which side of a street it is on. Paying close attention to local issues like parking, security, foot traffic, and complementary businesses will add a layer of specificity to your analysis.

Your reader needs this level of information and, as importantly, needs to know that you, as the operator of the business, have taken the time to dig down and get the ground truths which can make or break a retail operation. Digging down and getting the facts needed for this analysis will give you vital information you need to go forward with your project.

3.6 SWOT analysis

SWOT stands for Strengths, Weaknesses, Opportunities, Threats; SWOT is the initialism for a structured planning method which looks to identify the internal and external factors which will affect the success of a business. As an exercise in structured planning, SWOT gives a business owner a rubric which can direct analysis. From an investor or partner perspective, whether a fledgling business has done such an analysis is a useful clue as to the sophistication of the prospective owner.

A SWOT analysis can be as simple as making four lists in a notebook, or as complicated as running full-scale team analysis of each of the factors with input from your professional team and any consultants you are using.

It is possible, but usually undesirable, to produce a long form SWOT analysis that runs tens or even hundreds of pages and costs tens of thousands of dollars. However, for a start-up retail marijuana business, a short, to the point SWOT makes much more sense. See Sample 1 for an example.

The entire point of a SWOT analysis is to surface the factors which will affect the success or failure of the proposed business. By including a SWOT analysis in a business plan you are showing your potential investors, partners, and other readers that you have identified and thought through the issues. For an investor doing his or her due diligence before committing money to your business, the presence of a SWOT analysis ticks off one more box.

3.7 Industry background

Industry background is the section where you can put your proposed marijuana retail business into the context of the sweeping changes which have been occurring in the legal marijuana world in North America in the last few years. Where the business environment section needs to be local, factual, and data-driven, a short section talking about the Green Rush and the billions of dollars in the marijuana industry makes sense.

At the same time, writing a blue-sky scenario may, in fact, worry your audience rather than reassure them. Again, remember that a business plan is a marketing document and what you are marketing, along with your marijuana

Sample 1
SWOT Analysis for a Duncan, BC, Medical Marijuana Dispensary

Strengths (*characteristics of the business or project that give it an advantage over others*)

market town for 100,000 population Cowichan Valley; no current competition; low commercial rents in Duncan; several informal sources of high grade marijuana nearby; substantial markup available; low cost to open; option taken on premises which already has high security features; British Columbia pot-friendly jurisdiction; medical marijuana dispensaries generally tolerated in BC; $150,000 in ready money to invest; owner has previous retail experience; consultant retained from Vancouver who has opened nine dispensaries

Weaknesses (*characteristics that place the business or project at a disadvantage relative to others*)

medical marijuana dispensaries are illegal in Canada (federally); Duncan municipal council unwilling to grant business licenses to dispensaries at this time; informal sources of supply are potentially unreliable; very low barriers to competitive entry; owner has no experience with retail medical marijuana; location is in a problematic section of town

Opportunities (*elements that the business or project could exploit to its advantage*)

first mover advantage in local market; established dispensaries likely to be favored licensees when new Canadian regulations issued; bylaw enforcement in Duncan weak; significant expansion opportunity in three local towns (Lake Cowichan, Cowichan Bay, and Ladysmith); positioning for coming Canada-wide legalization of recreational marijuana

Threats (*elements in the environment that could cause trouble for the business or project*)

RCMP take dim view of retail marijuana; marijuana trafficking still Criminal Code offence in Canada; tax status of proceeds of sale of marijuana not determined; Duncan municipality has stated no business licenses will be issued in 2016 for retail marijuana; Cowichan Indian band exploring possibility of opening pot shop on nearby reservation land; difficulties in banking all cash business

retail business, is your own credibility. Pumping up the hype about the big Green Rush is gratifying, but a savvy investor already knows.

This is an opportunity to talk about what is not generally known about the retail marijuana business and why that matters to your particular business. For example, the legalization of recreational marijuana in Washington and Colorado led to oversupply conditions in the wholesale markets in both those states. That meant that prices for wholesale marijuana fell. If a similar trajectory occurs in your market, how would your business benefit?

Using an industry overview to showcase your own insights and awareness of the marketplace, the regulatory environment, and the rapid developments in both the product and the delivery modalities will tend to reassure potential investors and partners. It is an opportunity for you, as the owner operator, to look smart and well informed. Use it.

3.8 Operations plan

What are you going to do? How are you going to do it?

Walking through your plan, from your license application (or decision to proceed prior to licensing), to the securing of premises, to sourcing your marijuana and other goods for sale, to your employee hiring and on to issues such as security and banking demonstrates you have thought out your business operations.

In this section, put as many facts on paper as possible. If you have premises in mind, give the address. Are there key people you have already brought on board? Name them. If you are planning on buying your marijuana wholesale, name the wholesaler(s). Give some indication of the varietals you plan to stock. Will you open with dry marijuana only or will you have other options, like edibles and oils?

The key to a business operations section is specificity. Your reader needs to know you have thought through your operations and the best way to show you have is by giving chapter and verse on each phase of your proposed operations. You'll be discussing your costing in the financial sections but it is not a bad idea to include summary numbers in your operations section. What will it cost to open your doors? What will be the value of your stock on hand on day one? What are your total anticipated monthly running expenses? You'll break out those numbers in your financials but they are also a key part of your operational planning and therefore belong in this section.

3.9 Competitor analysis

Whether you are planning on opening your retail marijuana business in a jurisdiction where medical or recreational marijuana has been legal for some time or if you are planning on opening in a jurisdiction where legalization has just occurred or will occur shortly, you have competition.

First off, there is the competition from the black and grey marijuana markets. Legalization of medical and/or recreational marijuana does not wipe out the criminal element overnight. In fact, because legalization means that users are less concerned about being charged with possession, it may actually improve conditions for the illegal sellers. A degree of heavily taxed, tightly regulated legalization can be good for the underground marijuana market. Recognizing that fact is a good place to start your competitor analysis.

The second level of competitor analysis is to understand that where medical and recreational marijuana are both legal there is likely to be direct competition between the two sectors. This is due to the fact that medical marijuana dispensaries provide their product, in some jurisdictions, without the tax burden imposed on recreational pot shops. As gaining registered user status is relatively easy, heavy marijuana users may opt for the medical alternative.

The third level of analysis is direct competition between outlets with the same licensing. In the jurisdictions where recreational marijuana has been legalized, dozens of pot shops opened as quickly as they could be licensed. Marijuana dispensaries, where medical marijuana is legal, have increased in number as well. Many have operated in the same location for years.

Because you are looking at a retail marijuana business you will have a specific location in mind when you write your business plan. So it will make sense to view your competition locally. How many other marijuana outlets are there within a mile of your proposed location? Make a list and include it in your business plan. Then make a point of visiting each of your potential competitors and making notes. No two independent retail stores are the same, so pay attention to detail. Make note of pricing. Look for a standard marijuana product in a standard quantity and do price comparisons. Look at what else your potential competitors have for sale. Different preparations of marijuana? Different delivery systems? Get a sense of the look and feel, and spend some time watching the sorts of customers each competitor attracts. Simple characteristics like male or female; young, middle-aged, or older; hippie or hipster; driving, biking, walking; this will give you a feel for who is attracted to which establishment. Go online and look for each competitor's website. Take a look at their online marketing efforts. Do they run print advertising? Are they involved in the community?

If you can, find out who actually owns each business. Are they standalones or part of an ownership group? Where you can, try to determine each competitor's source of supply.

You will not get and do not need complete information about every one of your competitors, but being able to include a table in your business plan which lists all of them and has notes on each location is an impressive start. A potential investor or partner seeing that table and your notes will, once again, see that you have done your homework. (Which, by the way, will be very valuable as you proceed to design and open your own business.)

As well as looking locally, it is important to look at competitive trends within the industry in your jurisdiction and as a whole. For example, as legalization of recreational marijuana expands, individual pot shops have shown signs of consolidating or being bought out. As more recreational pot shops open there may be a tendency for growers at the wholesale level to concentrate on the production of a few bestselling, generic lines of pot. Will that change the competitive landscape for your proposed business? Once again, you do not have to have definitive answers to these questions; rather your business plan should reflect the fact you have looked at the competition.

3.10 Market analysis

A market analysis is about coming up with a realistic estimate of the size of your retail marijuana business's target market and understanding the composition of that market. A good market analysis will be data-driven and pay attention to what your most likely customers look like. It will then take a look at the location you have selected and come up with a demographic/psychographic profile of your particular area.

To do an accurate market analysis you need to have reached tentative decisions about your location and the look and feel of your store. If you are planning a medical marijuana dispensary you will likely be looking at a different target market from a recreational pot shop.

Who buys marijuana is your first question. You might get an answer to this question from market research conducted in jurisdictions where marijuana, medical or recreational, has been legalized. What you are looking for is data on who the users are — how old, gender, ethnicity, income group — and that data is not easy to find.

The second question is who lives in the area surrounding your proposed location? This data is easier to find because there is census data for every zip and postal code in the US and Canada. You can also, with a bit of searching, find free income data. For more interesting demographic/psychographic information, it is often worthwhile to get in touch with your local print media and ask for their media kit which will often have lots of demographic information about their circulation territory; the types of people who read their publications. (While you are there find out who the sales rep for your area is and say hi. Advertising salespeople often have a lot of information you are never going to find online. Besides, you'll probably be buying advertising so you may as well get the relationship off to a good start.)

Spend some time simply sitting where you can see your proposed location and watch the activity on the street. Take a look different days and at different times. You may want to do a formal traffic count, although that can be a prolonged process. While you are spending time in the neighborhood, speak to the store owners and managers nearby. What is the area like? How's business? Most people in retail are happy to talk.

For your market analysis you give the data you've found on medical or recreational marijuana users in general and then you look at your own research as to the composition of the area surrounding your location. What you are trying to achieve is not a perfect market study but rather a market analysis which will reassure a potential investor or partner that you have looked carefully at the available information and reached reasonable, data-supported conclusions as to the market viability of your retail marijuana business.

3.11 Marketing plan

A market analysis will indicate if the location you plan to use makes sense demographically; the fact there are lots of potential customers surrounding your retail marijuana business does not mean they are going to come to your store. They might but, without marketing, they might not.

Marketing is a huge topic and, within a business plan, a reader wants to see that the business owner has paid some attention to marketing concepts. There is no point in detailing every step of your marketing effort as you might do in a dedicated marketing plan. Instead, covering the high points is more than enough for the business plan. By covering the high points, you will also be setting up line items in your revenue and expense projections.

Marketing might seem to start with the name of your business. In fact, it starts several steps back from that. A retail store or a medical marijuana dispensary has a particular look and feel, a sensibility, a way of resonating with customers which creates a vibe or a tone for all that follows. On the retail continuum between Walmart and Nordstroms where do you see your business fitting: Are you designer cannabis or utility pot? Are you price-competitive or do you see your operation as delivering quality marijuana to knowledgeable customers at a premium price? Once you have figured out the look and feel you can come up with a name, a logo, and a design aesthetic. "Old Uncle Bert's Pot Emporium" will not work well as the name of a white and glass, upmarket store with the design aesthetic of a bottle of Chanel No. 5.

Making the fact you have considered look and feel a feature in your marketing plan will check another of the investor/partner boxes. Mentioning the name of a well-regarded designer as your go-to for that look and feel, while it instantly adds expense, also recognizes reality and helps your description.

From there the marketing plan goes to outreach: Putting the name of your business and what you are selling in front of people who want to buy your products. There is no right way to do this; instead a business plan needs to, briefly, outline your strategy and objectives in light of what your market analysis has told you about your location. Marketing can include everything from phone apps to websites to print ads, remembering always that there may be specific rules in your jurisdiction you have to follow. You may set up a referral program or a customer loyalty reward system. You might want to do very specific outreach into various communities you have determined are marijuana positive. You might want to do cross promotions with neighborhood businesses or sponsor community events. On the medical side, you might want to set up information sessions for seniors or demonstrations of vaporizers as an alternative medicine delivery system.

In your business plan you need to focus on what your marketing plan is for the duration of the time frame of the plan. That will give you a basis to include marketing costs in your financials.

3.12 Management summary

For an investor or potential partner or financier an essential question once the business case for your retail marijuana operation is understood is "Who is this person, and the rest of the management team? Are these the people I trust to achieve the goals in this business plan?"

If you are planning on being the sole owner/manager then the management summary needs to explain why you are the right person for the job. What is your business experience? Have you run a retail operation? Have you enjoyed success in other business ventures? Essentially, if this section is about you then it needs to set out what, exactly, you bring to the table.

More often, a management summary is about you as the founder and owner and your management team and, in the marijuana space, that team needs to include your lawyer and accountant. Where you are planning a straight retail operation with no grow operations then your team might only be yourself and a couple of managers plus your professional advisors.

A business plan is a marketing document. You want to put your team's accomplishments front and center. If your day manager has experience in the medical marijuana dispensary field it's important even if you are planning on opening a retail pot shop. Management positions in non-marijuana retail may be important; so are things such as business degrees and certificates.

Take a look at your draft operations plan. In that plan will be a whole variety of tasks from sourcing the goods for sale, to security, to information and accounting operations and on through to marketing, advertising, and outreach. Business plan readers keep a sharp eye out for missing pieces; if you have a section in operations on security they will want to see one of your managers having responsibility for security.

Including short business bios of your lawyer and accountant adds heft to the management summary. But what about the other people you will rely on to get your business open? Your graphic designer and your store designer will be critical to the look and feel of your store. What about your suppliers? While none of these people are, strictly speaking, management, they will be making significant contributions to your success.

One way to handle third parties in a management summary is with a simple "Key Third Parties" subsection. This will alert your reader to the quality of the people with whom you will be working most directly.

3.13 Financial plan

In Samples 2, 3, 4, and 5, (and available on the download kit), you will find a series of worksheets where you can take the numbers you have been compiling and start generating financial projections.

There are four worksheets which every business plan needs to include:

- **Income Statement**: This shows revenues, expenses, and profit for a given time period.

- **Cash Flow Projection**: This shows how cash is expected to flow in and out of your business.

- **Balance Sheet**: Presents a picture of your business's net worth at a particular point in time. It takes the financial data of your business and breaks it into three categories: assets, liabilities, and equity.

- **Start-Up Costs**: This covers the expenses you will incur setting up.

Creating these worksheets and walking through the projections is a key exercise for any start-up business, but it is not a financial plan. The raw numbers you are putting into your worksheets are the beginning, but there needs to be an analysis of why those numbers are right and why they will work.

Remember that a business plan is a marketing document and a credibility piece. Your reader needs to know how you have arrived at the numbers you have in your worksheet and needs to know that you have actually done the work to make those numbers as accurate as they can be.

In larger companies, when a set of financial statements is released it is almost always accompanied by notes as well as what is known as "management discussion and analysis" which provides full and complete disclosure of the company's performance and prospects in the view of that company's management. Developing notes and an MD & A for your projections will show your reader that you are on top of the financial projections you are presenting.

On your worksheets you will be providing estimates of expenses and revenues. Your reader will want to know how you arrived at those estimates. You will have done a lot of the preliminary legwork if you have worked through the preliminary business matters outlined in Chapter 2.

The first item in a financial plan is to indicate which numbers are hard numbers based on real quotes for your start-up expenses worksheet. A hard number is one where you have an accurate fix on a particular cost or, at least, a range for such a number. For example, if you have premises which you believe are suitable, you should be able to determine the monthly rental amount, the cost of leasehold improvements, and get a normal course quote for insurance. You will know exactly what the application fee is for the license(s) you require. You should be able to get quotes from your lawyer, accountant, and designer for their pre-opening fees. If you are buying your marijuana wholesale you will be able to get pricing from the wholesaler for your opening stock. Items such as store fixtures, packaging, point of sale equipment, inventory control software, and so on should come with set price tags. There are also items like opening advertising and marketing costs which are entirely within your control and therefore represent hard start-up costs.

Of the four worksheets, the Start-Up Costs Worksheet is going to have the most verifiable set of numbers. It will also need to contain a realistic line item for miscellaneous/other expenses and another line item for contingencies. The contingency number reflects the unforeseen on every one of the line items in the Start-Up cost sheet. Your reader does not want to see a huge number here; but a realistic 15–20 percent will be expected.

Your Start-up Costs Worksheet also will outline the source of funds which will pay for those costs. Here you need to answer the reader's question, "Where is the money coming from?"

There are a number of possible sources: your own resources, third party equity investors, loans. In writing your financial plan you need to remember that the retail marijuana business is heavily regulated as to sources of funds. Plus, as a general rule, conventional lenders such as banks and credit unions are unwilling to lend money to marijuana-based businesses. These facts, unique to the retail marijuana business, need to be acknowledged up front.

The remaining worksheets are about your business in operation. Your reader will want to see how you believe your business will do based on realistic assumptions. The question is, what is realistic? Your accountant can help you with the pro forma balance sheet, but the revenue and expenses and the cash flow projections are going to be based on your understanding of the business you are about to enter.

Entire books have been written on how to come up with realistic numbers for projected sales or expenses or operating margins. Models can be constructed and what-ifs run on spreadsheets, but there are really only two ways to come up with a coherent set of assumptions for your projections. The first is a bottom-up strategy of carefully estimating your operating expenses and cost of goods sold and then determining a breakeven sales figure, and then a sales figure which would provide a reasonable rate of return on investment. The second is a top-down exercise where you determine what rate of return you require and then look at what that means for sales and expenses. It makes sense to consider both methods as you work on projections, however, the bottom-up method is where you will likely start because the hard numbers lie in your costs.

Sample 2
Income and Expenses Worksheet

Income	
Income	
Total Monthly Income	$6,000.00
Expenses	
Advertising	$150.00
Bank service charges	$22.00
Credit card payments	
Shipping charges	
Electricity	$220.00
Health insurance	$100.00
Heating	
Insurance	$100.00
Internet	$60.00
Inventory replenishment	
Lease payments	$1,000.00
Loan payments	$500.00
Office supplies	$35.00
Payroll	$2,500.00
Payroll taxes	$500.00
Professional association fees	$50.00
Rent	
Repairs and maintenance	
Sales tax	
Telephone	$50.00
Security	$513.50
Public relations	
Web presence	$20.00
Regulatory compliance	$150.00
Professional fees	
Other: _____	
Other: _____	
Other: _____	
Other: _____	
Other: _____	
Total	$5,970.50

Total Income Minus Expenses $29.50

Sample 3
Cash Flow Projections Worksheet

	Month 1	Month 2	Month 3	Month 4	Month 5	Month 6	Month 7	Month 8	Month 9	Month 10	Month 11	Month 12	Annual
Sales													
Marijuana	100,000	107,000	114,000	121,000	128,000	130,000	130,000	130,000	130,000	130,000	130,000	130,000	1,480,000
Accessories	25,000	26,750	28,500	30,250	32,000	32,500	32,500	32,500	32,500	32,500	32,500	32,500	370,000
Gross	125,000	133,750	142,500	151,250	160,000	162,500	162,500	162,500	162,500	162,500	162,500	162,500	1,850,000
	50,000	53,500	57,000	60,500	64,000	65,000	65,000	65,000	65,000	65,000	65,000	65,000	740,000
Net Sales	75,000	80,250	85,500	90,750	96,000	97,500	97,500	97,500	97,500	97,500	97,500	97,500	1,110,000
Expenses													
Advertising	1,000	1,000	1,000	1,000	1,000	1,000	1,000	1,000	1,000	1,000	1,000	1,000	12,000
Bank service charges	100	100	100	100	100	100	100	100	100	100	100	100	1,200
Credit card payments	1,875	2,006	2,138	2,269	2,400	2,438	2,438	2,438	2,438	2,438	2,438	2,438	27,750
Shipping charges	500	500	500	500	500	500	500	500	500	500	500	500	6,000
Electricity	500	500	500	500	500	500	500	500	500	500	500	500	6,000
Health insurance	3,000	3,000	3,000	3,000	3,000	3,000	3,000	3,000	3,000	3,000	3,000	3,000	36,000
Heating	300	300	300	300	300	300	300	300	300	300	300	300	3,600
Insurance	600	600	600	600	600	600	600	600	600	600	600	600	7,200
Internet	100	100	100	100	100	100	100	100	100	100	100	100	1,200
Inventory replenishment	50,000	53,500	57,000	60,500	64,000	65,000	65,000	65,000	65,000	65,000	65,000	65,000	740,000
Lease payments	3,000	3,000	3,000	3,000	3,000	3,000	3,000	3,000	3,000	3,000	3,000	3,000	36,000
Loan payments	0	0	0	0	0	0	0	0	0	0	0	0	0
Office supplies	100	100	100	100	100	100	100	100	100	100	100	100	1,200
Payroll	10,000	10,000	10,000	10,000	10,000	10,000	10,000	10,000	10,000	10,000	10,000	10,000	120,000
Payroll taxes	700	700	700	700	700	700	700	700	700	700	700	700	8,400
Professional association fees	100	100	100	100	100	100	100	100	100	100	100	100	1,200
Rent													0
Repairs and maintenance	500	500	500	500	500	500	500	500	500	500	500	500	6,000
Sales tax													0
Telephone	100	100	100	100	100	100	100	100	100	100	100	100	1,200
Security	3,000	3,000	3,000	3,000	3,000	3,000	3,000	3,000	3,000	3,000	3,000	3,000	36,000
Public relations	1,200	1,200	1,200	1,200	1,200	1,200	1,200	1,200	1,200	1,200	1,200	1,200	14,400
Web presence	500	500	500	500	500	500	500	500	500	500	500	500	6,000
Regulatory compliance	1,500	1,500	1,500	1,500	1,500	1,500	1,500	1,500	1,500	1,500	1,500	1,500	18,000
Professional fees	3,000	3,000	3,000	3,000	3,000	3,000	3,000	3,000	3,000	3,000	3,000	3,000	36,000
Total Expenses	81,675	85,306	88,938	92,569	96,200	97,238	97,238	97,238	97,238	97,238	97,238	97,238	1,125,350
													0
Profit/Loss	-6,675	-5,056	-3,438	-1,819	-200	262.5	262.5	262.5	262.5	262.5	262.5	262.5	-15,350

Sample 3 – Continued

An ongoing business operation has costs every day. Rent, insurance, property taxes, salaries, utilities, security, advertising, professional services: These are bills to be paid just to keep the doors open. Most of those costs can be captured on a revenue and expenses statement as hard numbers and those numbers will not vary greatly with your sales volume. If you do well you may have to hire more people, if you miss your numbers you may have to trim the headcount; but the rest of the numbers are pretty much fixed.

Cost of Goods Sold where you are buying from a wholesaler would appear fixed: If a pound of pot costs $1,000 that would seem to be the COGS. However, added to the wholesale cost of the marijuana are items such as packaging, spoilage, waste, theft. These may not seem like much, but even a 10 percent additional cost can hit your profits hard.

The magic of retail lies in the ability to mark up the wholesale price of the products you sell. So, in doing your projections, you have to come up with a markup. Critically, from that markup you have to cover your operating expenses and your profit.

When you are trying to come up with a markup number you are constrained by two things: first, the minimum return on investment, i.e., profit, which makes sense for your retail marijuana business and second, the competitive environment.

In practical terms, you cannot price your marijuana for a great deal more than the medical marijuana dispensary on the next block or the pot shop five blocks away. Here the issue is that when marijuana is legalized in a particular jurisdiction it fairly quickly becomes a commodity with a market price set largely by the competitive forces in that jurisdiction.

A business plan promising a 45 percent ROI that is based on selling marijuana at twice the going retail price is a recipe for disaster. A business plan

Sample 4
Balance Sheet Worksheet

Date:

ASSETS

Current Assets	Value
Cash on Hand	
Petty Cash	
Cash in Bank	
Inventory on Hand	
Accounts Receivable	
A: Total Current Assets	
Fixed Assets	
Real Estate, Land	
Real Estate, Buildings	
Original Cost	
Less Reserve for Depreciation	
Furniture and Fixtures	
Original Cost	
Less Reserve for Depreciation	
Motor Vehicle, Machinery	
Original Cost	
Less Reserve for Depreciation	
B: Total Fixed Assets	B $
Other Assets	
C: Total Other Assets	C $
D: TOTAL ASSETS [D = A + B + C]	D $

LIABILITIES

Current Liabilities	Value
Accounts Payable	
Notes Payable	
Taxes Payable	
E: Total Current Liabilities	E $
Other Liabilities	
F: Total Other Liabilities	F $
G: TOTAL LIABILITIES [G = E + F]	G $

NET WORTH	
H: Net Worth = Assets - Liabilities	H $

Sample 5
Start-up Costs Worksheet

License Expenses	
Professional Fees re: License	
Lease	
Security and Surveillance	
Beginning Inventory	
Branding	
Signage	
Packaging	
Advertising	
POS Equipment	
Computer Equipment	
Software	
Construction	
Furniture	
Fixtures and Equipment	
Decorating	
Advertising	
Opening Expenses	
Cash Float	
Office Supplies	
Installation and Setup	
Website/Social Media	
Contingency	
Other: _____	
Other: _____	
Other: _____	
Other: _____	
Other: _____	
Total	$0.00

which achieves a modest return on investment selling pot at the average market price is the beginning of a successful venture.

Margins

What does an attractive margin look like? A typical Subway sandwich franchise in Canada sees net margins of 20 percent on average sales of around $8,000 CAD a week, with a cost to open the store in the neighborhood of $130,000 to $180,000 CAD.

Can a retail marijuana business see those sorts of numbers? The short answer is yes. In Colorado, in 2015, recreational marijuana sales worth $587,834,219 were made by a combined 424 recreational pot stores: That is an average of $1,386,401 per store or just over $115,000 per month.

If those Colorado stores are seeing the same net margin as an average Subway, their owners would be seeing $22,000 a month in profit. But are they?

Because of the way in which the IRS has interpreted the law many of these businesses are unable to deduct the normal costs of doing business which means that they are being taxed on their sales without being able to deduct rent, salaries, and so on. The effect of this is to drive the net margins of marijuana retailers down. In fact, in some cases, successful retail marijuana businesses have a net loss after tax.

☘ ☘ ☘

The financial planning section of your business plan needs to balance credibility and hard numbers with the opportunities which the retail marijuana business offers. It needs to recognize the dynamic nature of the particular jurisdiction. For example, starting up in a jurisdiction where medical and recreational marijuana have been legal for some time presents a different SWOT profile from a jurisdiction which is just getting ready to legalize.

Your pro forma income/expense, cash flow projection, and balance sheet worksheets need to present a baseline case where you provide an entirely realistic set of numbers. However, there is no reason not to add a set of projections with what might be termed upside surprises. In particular, if you are in the United States, running the numbers where the IRS changes its position as to the deductibility of normal course business expenses makes a great deal of sense. As does a set of projections where the wholesale price of marijuana declines over time, as has been the experience in Washington and Colorado since legalization.

In addition to these optimistic alternative cases, you may also want to pay attention to factors you believe will set your store apart from your competitors and either increase sales volume or margin or, ideally, both. Which brings us to another worksheet: Advertising, Marketing, and Promotion.

One of the essential determinants of business success in a competitive market is establishing a brand presence in that market. Everything from signage to packaging to the Internet to print advertising will help establish that presence. While there may be three line items on your expense sheet for advertising, marketing, and promotion, it is important to break out the costs for the business plan reader. Adding a worksheet makes this possible.

The financial plan is the platform upon which the rest of the business plan rests. Each line item on your expense sheet ties directly back to a point you will have made in your plan. Your projections for revenue, expenses, and cash flow demonstrate your capacity to understand the retail marijuana business in sufficient detail to actually open and run such a business.

Your financial plan is essential. It may take a while to research and write, but every hour you spend will increase the chances of your success.

3.14 Attachments and milestones

Attachments are really a way of adding substance to your business plan. For example, if you have a location in mind it does not hurt to include pictures of the location and the neighborhood. If you have a floor plan of the space with your proposed leasehold improvements and fixtures, that will add weight. Do you have a logo? Package design? Attachments will add reality to your plan.

If you are adding attachments, make sure you reference them in the business plan. Make it easy for your reader. Some plans will include the CVs of the management and the advisors as part of the attachment package.

Milestones are just that: Dates by which specific things will be achieved. However, because the start date of your project is subject to such things as the issue of a license and securing financing, it may make sense to set up you milestones from a specific event, i.e., 30 days from license issue, 60 days, and so on. If you encounter a delay at the start, your milestones would be adjusted accordingly.

Make sure your milestones align with your financial projections. Again, remember that an investor or prospective partner reading your plan will notice if your projections call for breakeven in month three from opening but your milestones say month six.

3.15 Exit and/or succession strategy

Even as you are planning to start a business you should be considering how you will leave it. This is important if you are the sole investor in the business and even more important if there are other investors.

Typically, looking five years ahead is about as far as a preliminary business plan can usefully project. In those projections there will be an indication of the value of the equity in the business and what the value of owning that business is at each stage of its growth. In the early years the equity value of the business is likely to be negative. That's why you need capital to get your business started and to subsidize it as it grows, but at some point, ideally quite soon after you open for business, revenues will exceed expenses and the equity position will move from negative to positive. This may mean cash in the bank or it may mean you reduce the outstanding amounts invested in the business; either way the value of the business as a going concern increases over time where you have net revenue.

A brief discussion of your exit options or succession plan in your business plan shows that you are serious about the whole life cycle of the business. You do not have to be terribly specific but you can certainly make the statement that you plan to, annually, review the strategic options available to your business.

Some of the original recreational marijuana stores in Colorado have been put up for sale by their original owners. Including the possibility of sale in your business plan gives investors at least one clear path to seeing the return of their capital.

Marijuana: A Primer

4

Getting ready to sell marijuana at retail involves developing product knowledge. There are terrific online resources on marijuana strains. You can start with Leafy.com or look up marijuana on YouTube. You can also look online for specific strains for a more granular approach to the extraordinary variety of marijuana hybrids.

However, a little bit of information before you start your detailed research will let you find the knowledge you need more quickly. So, a short primer.

1. Potted History

Cannabis, known more commonly as marijuana or marihuana, is a mildly psychoactive substance that has been cultivated since, at least, sometime between 3000 and 2000 BCE, and likely significantly before then (there are recorded uses of hemp as fibre as early as 10000 BCE, however, I am more concerned with cannabis as medicine).

The medicinal use of cannabis has a long history — thousands of years — across a variety of cultures. The first recorded use of cannabis as medicine was in a book by Emperor Shen-Nung in 2737 BCE, where he recommended its use for gout, rheumatoid arthritis, stomach problems, and difficulty concentrating. In Chinese herbology, it is considered one of the 50 essential herbs. In Egypt, cannabis suppositories were recorded from 1550 BCE to treat hemorrhoids. In ancient India, cannabis was used to treat many symptoms that it is used to treat today (more on this in section 2.): insomnia, pain, headaches, and stomach issues. The ancient Greeks used cannabis to treat nosebleeds, and used the seeds to force the expulsion of tapeworms. The ancient Muslim world used it for all of the above-mentioned medicinal purposes from the eighth century CE.

Modern medicinal cannabis was first conceptualized, and introduced to the West, in the nineteenth century by William Brooke O'Shaughnessy, an Irish physician whose work with the East India Trading Company brought him in direct contact with Cannabis Indica. He observed that cannabis resin reduced suffering and spasticity in patients with tetanus, and its ability to reduce spasms and inflammation in infants.

2. Current Medical Uses

Albert Lockhart and Manley West conducted further research during the 1960s, and by 1987 they had received a patent as well as legal permission to distribute Canasol, one of the first marijuana extracts. Marinol — a synthetic version of THC — was approved by the FDA in the 1970s for treatment of chemotherapy-induced nausea and vomiting and for the treatment of anorexia brought on by AIDS.

Currently, cannabis is used to treat a plethora of symptoms and conditions, depending on which strains are being used and their ratios of active cannabinoids. The symptoms most commonly cited, and for which there is the most proof of the efficacy of cannabis, are chemotherapy-induced nausea and vomiting, reduced appetite due to AIDS or other conditions, chronic pain, spasticity, and, recently, in the treatment of seizures. Insomnia, as well as anxiety, PTSD, and various other psychological disorders are often cited, however, other than in the case of insomnia, the results can be paradoxical (e.g., cannabis causes anxiety in some people).

Current research has shown some potential for cannabis to have anticarcinogenic effects, however, smoking cannabis has also been shown to release many carcinogens and as such, another ingestion method would likely be required to reap the benefits of these studies. Fortunately, many other ingestion methods exist. Further research is being conducted into cannabis' effects on glaucoma, epilepsy, diabetes, and dementia — most of which is based on the anecdotes of patients suffering from these conditions for whom cannabis provided some relief. There are many anecdotal reports of the efficacy of cannabis for the treatment of irritable bowel syndrome and other gastrointestinal issues ranging from anxiety-related diarrhea all the way through to Crohn's disease.

3. Types and Effects

Psychoactive cannabis can be broken down into two species: Cannabis Indica and Cannabis Sativa, as well as hundreds-to-thousands of different strains (roughly equivalent to breeds). Typically, strains of the sativa breed will be high in the cannabinoid THC (delta-9-tetrahydrocannabinol) and lower in CBD (cannabidiol), and are thought to be more medically useful in promoting appetite, creative thinking, and concentration. These strains are, in recreational terms, ones that provide a giddy, up-type "high." Conversely, indica strains are typically higher in CBD and lower in THC, often used for pain reduction, treatment of gastrointestinal problems, and insomnia.

In recreational terms, the effects of these strains are described as a mellow, "couch-lock," "stoned" feeling as opposed to the "giddy high" of sativas. It must be pointed out, however, that these are just typical, not absolute, standards. There are, in particular, a large number of indica and indica-dominant strains that are incredibly high in THC and vice-versa. As well, while higher-CBD strains tend to result in a more stoned feeling, strains that have little to no THC tend not to produce intoxicating effects at all, so further research is required to learn the interaction between THC and CBD in order to figure out why a strain with 0.5 percent THC, and 19 percent CBD produces almost no intoxication, but a strain with 10 percent THC and 19 percent CBD produces a stoned effect, and a strain with 19 percent THC and 10 percent CBD produces a high effect.

Finding purely indica or sativa strains is increasingly rare. This is because of the advent of crossbreeding of species to produce hybrid strains. As a side effect of failure of very low THC-content pot to produce any sort of a high, some breeding between indica and sativa was required in order to produce the intoxicating effects desired by many users. While it is possible for a pure indica to have high THC content, it is much easier to consistently produce high THC content when you breed with a sativa.

Different strains of medical marijuana, where the intent is not to produce intoxication, are used for different conditions. Conditions calling for indica are predominantly treated with indica-dominant hybrids. Likewise, though not as necessarily, conditions that are typically treated with sativa are usually treated with a sativa-dominant hybrid.

However, because it is not as necessary to have CBD present, and because some people don't like the couch-locking effect of CBD heavy strains, it is more common to find a pure sativa than it is to find a pure indica. However, the opposite is also true in terms of preference. Those predisposed to anxiety tend to find pure indica strains preferential to hybrids, even indica-dominant hybrids, because the "high" effect of sativas tends to exacerbate their anxiety condition. This tends to result in well-supplied dispensaries' stock being 85 percent hybrids, 10 percent pure sativa, and 5 percent pure indica.

There are situations, however, that call for CBD heavy strains with almost no THC; typically, in the treatment of children where preferential treatments have been ineffective. Due to the moral and medical implications of intoxicated children, parents, rightly, do not want their children to be treated with tinctures or extracts or edibles that have the potential for intoxication. The typically cited strain is "Charlotte's Web," named after a young girl who suffered 300 grand mal seizures a week, with no improvement from traditional treatment methods, only to have significant improvement after using marijuana tinctures of a particular strain that had 0.5 percent THC and up to 19 percent CBD contents. These strains are typically not stocked by the ad hoc Canadian dispensaries but they are fairly common in places like Colorado.

As the medical use of cannabis becomes more mainstream, the impact of low THC marijuana is becoming more pronounced. Research is becoming clearer that there are significant medicinal benefits for children from these low THC hybrids, with greatly reduced harm. (A significant consideration as research also shows that cannabis use in childhood or adolescence has negative effects that do not exist in usage that started in adulthood).

4. Alternatives to Smoking Marijuana

In terms of consumption, recreational marijuana is typically combusted and smoked, which, while medically beneficial, creates medical problems of its own, namely the release of a significant number of carcinogens. With the advent of legal or quasi-legal medical marijuana, other ingestion methods have been developed (some of which existed in the recreational world before, but accounted for a tiny minority of total consumption).

Extracts as well as plant material can be "vaporized," which involves heating the material enough to release the active ingredients, but not hot enough for it to combust. Edibles, as the name suggests, are foodstuffs that have been infused with marijuana and thus do not present the same carcinogenic effects of combustion. Tinctures are similar to edibles in that they can be ingested, but they can also be applied topically.

These methods have greatly reduced the medical side effects related to combustion, but come with problems of their own; dosage is more difficult to control, and inexperienced users can overdo it and experience unwanted side effects, typically over-intoxication. With appropriate instruction from qualified distributors, these effects are greatly mitigated, and the benefits of the new ingestion methods far outweigh the occasional "paranoid, bad trip" experienced by an inexperienced user who "dabs" (cultural term for vaporizing extracts) too much extract or eats one too many pot brownies.

5. Marijuana Cultivation, Harvest, Drying, and Curing

As a marijuana retailer, whether medicinal or recreational, you may choose to, or be required by regulation, to grow some, or all, of your marijuana product. These requirements are being relaxed in many of the jurisdictions that first imposed them because the jurisdictions are recognizing that the skill sets of expert growers are often very different from those of retailers.

If you are not growing your own, you are sourcing from an authorized grower on a wholesale basis. As a retailer, you need to have some idea of what to look for and what to watch out for when buying your product.

Marijuana cultivation is a fascinating blend of farming, science, and art. There are no absolute rules. Some growers prefer to begin each plant from a seed, others will prefer the breeding certainty that a propagated clone gives them. In some environments the "garden" will be outdoors, others will be indoors. Some will grow without pesticides and follow organic practices, others will use pesticides and nearly industrial farming methods.

In every case, growers will be looking for maximum yield but that yield can come with compromises. As a buyer you may not care about the compromises, only about the price, or you may not care about the price as long as few compromises were made in the growing process.

There are a few facts about growing marijuana that are near certain. One, outdoor-grown product will always be of an inferior quality to indoor-grown product (due generally to the ability to control variables during a growing cycle). Two, organic product, while not necessarily inferior, will always yield less than product grown with non-organic methods (e.g., chemical fertilizers, pesticides, etc.). Three, outdoor product is typically organic — "organic outdoor" is a bit of a misnomer because it's rare anyone growing outdoors is using major industrial farming methods — this may change as the legal status of marijuana cultivation does.

These facts mean that you will typically pay more for organic product of equal quality. This is basic economics: The labor cost is the same but the yield is less, so that cost needs to be made up somewhere. They also mean that outdoor pot, at least as currently cultivated, might actually cost more than indoor pot of the same inferior quality; there is actually more labor that goes into outdoor crops than indoor crops, and so, after initial start-up costs, indoor becomes the far more economically viable product.

Organic and inorganic aside, indoor product is typically grown one of two ways: in soil, or hydroponically. Once hydroponics are set up, they are simple, effective, and produce massive yields, but typically, there is a limit on quality. Soil requires years to learn how to produce maximum quality and maximum yields. Once that expertise is gained, it is typically the way to go.

In any event, after several weeks to several months of growing, followed by several more weeks of flowering, the product is harvested. Much of marijuana's pre-combustion "sensible qualities" — taste and smell, particularly — are actually developed after harvest. While poor post-harvest practices won't usually affect quality (assuming the marijuana wasn't left to mold), they will affect marketability. Because of this, it is essential for a retailer to have a grower that properly dries the marijuana — typically, by hanging it in a dark, dry, well ventilated, sterile environment — and then properly cures the marijuana (by leaving it in sealed containers in the same environment). The curing process, in particular, is where taste and smell are developed, but if one attempts to cure marijuana without properly drying it, mold ensues.

With all of this in mind, the grower should be an expert. This faces the would-be retailer with the prospect of identifying an expert grower. Furthermore, for licensing reasons, the expert grower can't have a criminal record. Given marijuana's until recently illegal status, this presents a challenge.

The best way to identify an expert is to ask about practices and gauge expertise as you go — does he grow outdoors? Probably not an expert. Is she using hydroponics? She might be an expert, but might not be; ask to see photos of her grow-room (most growers are more than happy to do this, though many can be hesitant to give onsite tours for security reasons). If his setup has five plants, he's not an expert. If it's not a fairly sanitary, and well- ventilated environment, she's not an expert. If the walls are neither white nor reflective, not an expert. A lot of information can be gleaned from a visual inspection of a grower's operation, even by the layperson via photos.

Finally, before you even bother interviewing prospective wholesalers/ growers, insist on a criminal background check; the guy could have been growing triple A pot for the last 25 years, but there's no point in knowing that if he can't grow it for you legally.

The Legal Situation

In many ways this chapter could be placed at the front of this book. However, rather than tying you in legal knots from the beginning, it makes more sense to understand the legal issues surrounding marijuana in the context of business risk rather than as a stand-alone issue.

Every business operates within a legal system. Every legal system both creates and contains business risk and the marijuana business is no different. However, selling marijuana also brings with it unique legal issues which depend on jurisdiction.

Because every jurisdiction's laws regarding the sale of medical or recreational marijuana are different it is vital that you seek competent legal advice at the earliest stage of planning your marijuana retail operation. Do not rely on this book or this chapter for the detailed knowledge only a lawyer familiar with marijuana and business laws in your area can bring to your business.

A business risk approach to your legal situation leaves the law itself to your lawyers and gives you the tools to understand and deal with the impact of your legal situation on your business.

1. Understanding the State of the Law

It is very easy to get bogged down in legal and regulatory details because it is those details which matter in setting up your marijuana retail business. But looking at the state of the law will help you to assess the business implications of the legal advice you need to get.

The opening position in the United States and in Canada is that under federal law in both countries, the possession and sale of marijuana is illegal. In the United States, marijuana is a Schedule I substance under the 1970 Controlled Substances Act. In Canada, marijuana is a Schedule II substance under the 1996 *Controlled Drugs and Substances Act*.

In both countries, the possession or sale of marijuana is controlled by the federal criminal law. However, in the US, various states have taken less punitive approaches, making simple possession of small amounts of marijuana a misdemeanor offence; basically a traffic ticket. In Canada, depending on location, adult possession of small amounts of marijuana is routinely ignored by the police and even where an arrest is made, Crown Counsel (Canada's equivalent to an Assistant District Attorney), will rarely take the charges to Court.

2. Decriminalization versus Legalization

In simple terms, formal or informal decriminalization means that possession, cultivation, and sale of marijuana no longer attracts criminal penalties. Formal decriminalization would mean actually changing the law regarding marijuana so that those criminal penalties no longer exist. Informal decriminalization can range from the police de-prioritizing marijuana crimes through to jurisdictions allowing the sale of marijuana under certain circumstances.

In the US, the most obvious examples of formal decriminalization are the many state level efforts to allow marijuana to be sold for medical purposes and/or decide to allow the sale of marijuana for recreational use. These initiatives do not change the federal laws against marijuana, however the Federal government has indicated — by way of the Cole Memorandum of August 29, 2013 — that where states pass legislation which regulate the sale and distribution of marijuana the Federal government will not prosecute in the absence of evidence of involvement of organized crime or the violation of seven other enforcement goals. If you are in the US and contemplating entering the marijuana business you need to read the Cole Memorandum; a link can be found in the download kit.

Millions and millions of dollars have been invested in the marijuana industry in the United States based on the Cole Memorandum. From a business perspective, many investors have decided that the federal government's agreement to forebear from criminal prosecution is enough security to proceed. It is interesting that federally regulated banks and the IRS did not see the Cole Memorandum as legalizing the sale of marijuana.

What the Cole Memorandum does do is require a state level regulatory scheme consistent with its stated objectives and the compliance of marijuana operations with that regulatory scheme. From the business perspective, what this means is that noncompliance with a state level regulatory scheme, as well as exposing a business to license revocation and other state sanctions, may draw the attention of federal prosecutors.

Legalization is not the same as decriminalization. If marijuana was descheduled from the Controlled Substances Acts in Canada and the US it would not be regulated or taxed in any way as the result of such rescheduling. It would have the same legal status as chocolate bars and soft drinks.

Legalization — as a direct result of the Cole Memorandum in the US as well as various international treaties — continues to treat marijuana as a controlled substance, but regulates and taxes its sale. This is a critical fact when you are considering entering the marijuana business at any level in the US. Where marijuana is legalized it is regulated and taxed.

The degree to which marijuana is regulated varies between jurisdictions. In Colorado, the entire system is designed to regulate the product from seed to sale and identify and vet the people handling the product. It is a closed system. In Washington, along with regulations governing production and sale, there are extensive regulations going to advertising and promotion.

Canada's abortive attempts to regulate the production and sale of medical marijuana were premised on a closed system whereby licensed growers could only sell to certified medical users with delivery taking place by mail. The courts made short work of this but not before several hundred million dollars had been raised in the public marketplace for what were essentially government-sanctioned, industrial scale grow-ops.

3. Business Risk and the State of the Law

If you find yourself in a jurisdiction where medical and recreational marijuana have been legalized you are in a position to assess with some accuracy the business risks involved. Essentially, you have to calculate what the costs will be of complying with the regulations in your jurisdiction. If there is a mandated inventory control system, what will it cost? What are the costs of the required security systems?

In these situations the only option is to comply with the regulations and licensing requirements. So the business decision hinges on whether you can make money while in compliance. Because the regulations are in place you should have no surprises and your cost calculations will, like most cost calculations, be close enough to let you decide whether to proceed.

Knowing what is required for compliance from an early stage will let you minimize your compliance costs by selecting premises which can be easily adapted, ensuring that required safe rooms and entry checks are capable of being built without violating building codes, ensuring key hires meet the licensing requirements if any and developing policies and practices which are in compliance from the beginning.

Where things become more difficult are in jurisdictions where marijuana is not yet legalized and regulated, or where only medical marijuana is regulated. In the United States at the time of writing, we were in the middle of the elections of 2016 and there were up to ten states where some form of marijuana legalization will be on the ballot. In Canada, the current government has promised legalization legislation for 2017.

As a business proposition, positioning a retail marijuana operation for potential legalization looks like a risk. After all, it is difficult to know if a ballot measure will be passed and equally difficult to know how long it will take a state legislature to pass the required legislation and even more difficult to know what the regulations under that legislation will look like. At the same time, the opportunity presented by legalization can be huge. As a first mover in a new jurisdiction, a retail pot shop can have lineups around the block and establish brand and reputation very quickly.

The fact that there are conditions of political and regulatory uncertainty definitely changes the business risk calculation. However, against that is the fact that the upfront cost of preparation for eventual legalization is relatively low. Hiring a lawyer; scouting some locations; perhaps putting out requests for proposals for graphics and the website; lining up financing; and building a file for the license application process do not involve significant costs.

Plus, and this is likely important, we now know that the regulatory regimes in Colorado and Washington pass the Cole Memorandum test as these regulatory regimes have not been challenged by the federal Department of Justice. On that basis, and on the basis that Oregon has adopted a hybrid of the Washington and Colorado regulatory systems, it is a reasonable bet that your state's regulations will be similar to the existing systems. Creating a different regulatory system from scratch may occur in California for medical marijuana but this has as much to do with uniquely Californian conditions as with any desire to reinvent the regulatory wheel.

Again, the business risk of a political failure to legalize or regulations which are more onerous than the Colorado closed system combined with the license number cap and advertising restrictions of Washington does exist but can be discounted. A business planning exercise in an American jurisdiction which is likely to legalize recreational marijuana in the next electoral cycle, which uses the Colorado model as its base case regulatory model, is not likely to be too far wrong. Given the potential reward this could be a very clever business move.

Because of the Cole Memorandum and the regulatory experience in Colorado and other states, the business risk involved in preparing for legalization in an American jurisdiction can be calculated and built into your business plan.

Those in Canada face much greater uncertainty and therefore risk.

4. Canada, Oh Canada

The situation in Canada is complex and deeply uncertain. On the one hand we have the promise of legalization of marijuana in 2017. On the other we have the failed medical marijuana regulatory scheme decisively thrown out by the courts in early 2016. In the ensuing vacuum, in Vancouver and other pot-friendly municipalities, unregulated marijuana dispensaries catering to "medical" marijuana customers have sprung up, and we have a potential collision of the federal and provincial governments as to how marijuana is to be sold in the event of its legalization. Plus, because of all of the above, no system of regulation is an obvious model going forward.

At the moment, in Canada, possession and sale is illegal except in the case of medical marijuana. The original medical marijuana regulations allowed personal growing of marijuana for medical purposes and required an "Authorization to Possess" certificate which, in turn, required what was, in effect, a prescription from a doctor. These regulations were changed in 2013 to eliminate the right to personally grow or designate a grower and replace that system with licensed growers and mail-order delivery. And those new regulations only dealt with "dried marijuana."

The medical marijuana regulations were found unconstitutional in federal court in February 2014, in the Allard decision. The Supreme Court of Canada found that the dried marijuana restriction was also unconstitutional in 2015, in the Smith decision. The federal government has indicated it will not be appealing. This means that the federal government had until August of 2016 to come up with regulations regarding medical marijuana which can survive constitutional scrutiny. They have reinstated the right of registered medical marijuana users to grow their own marijuana or to designate a grower. They have not, however, authorized retail dispensaries selling to registered medical marijuana users leaving grey market dispensaries out of the medical marijuana regulatory scheme.

The new federal government under Trudeau was elected in 2015. One of his promises was to legalize the recreational use of marijuana. On April 20, 2016 — 4/20, so no one can deny Trudeau has a sense of humor — the

Minister of Health announced that there would be a task force appointed to look into every element of the legalization of marijuana and that, after the report of that task force, legislation to legalize would be introduced in the spring of 2017 (possibly on 4/20/2017).

Canadian marijuana entrepreneurs have not waited for the courts, Health Canada or Parliament; instead they have opened hundreds of marijuana "dispensaries" operating for profit behind a rather broad view of who is entitled to purchase medical marijuana and what documentation is required. A 60-second Skype assessment by a naturopath in which anything from sleep trouble to a sore back will yield a "Medical Document" can mean a purchaser is good to go.

All of this has led to chaos in the Canadian marijuana marketplace. The large scale federally licensed, often publicly traded, medical marijuana grow-ops are not allowed to sell to the ad hoc dispensaries and are demanding they be shut down. The police in many jurisdictions have taken a hands-off approach. The regulation of the dispensaries has become, by default, a municipal issue. (The City of Vancouver takes a licensing and zoning approach which is leading to the closure of many of the city's more than 100 dispensaries; that, and a $30,000 yearly business license fee.) In response to public complaints, police in Toronto have taken a very hands-on approach, raiding more than 40 storefront medical dispensaries and laying 186 charges.

The chaos is likely to continue for some time. The medical marijuana regulations due in August 2016 may clarify the situation somewhat; however, they are almost certainly going to be subject to a court challenge if they are even slightly restrictive. The federal task force appears to have a very broad mandate which will likely mean it will be late with its report.

Assessing the legal situation from a business risk perspective is difficult. Adding to that difficulty is the perennial problem of Canadian constitutional issues; which level of government is entitled to make the rules regarding the sale of recreational marijuana. The federal government has jurisdiction over criminal law and has used that jurisdiction to carve out the exemption for medical marijuana. However, if recreational marijuana is decriminalized in the sense of no longer being subject to the criminal law, it is not obvious that the federal government will have any constitutional capacity to regulate its sale. This would mean sale of marijuana would be regulated by the provinces and would almost certainly result in a patchwork of regulatory regimes across the country. Even if marijuana remains a scheduled drug there will be a good deal of pressure on the federal government to allow the provinces to regulate the sale of marijuana.

The marijuana entrepreneurs who have been opening dispensaries across Canada have done their own risk assessments and concluded that there is money to be made amidst the chaos. Many of them have contacted law enforcement in their jurisdictions and found that while the police will tell them marijuana remains illegal in Canada, so long as they do not sell to minors, they will not be a law enforcement priority. So, in the hundreds, dispensaries are springing up without any regulation at all. In fact, the biggest constraint seems to be the municipal governments' willingness to issue business licenses to these ad hoc dispensaries. Some municipalities will, some will not, and some are adopting a wait and see attitude.

Unlike in the US, if you want to open a retail marijuana shop legally anywhere in Canada there is simply no way to determine the rules or even the likely rules under which you will be required to operate. For many, that has been an invitation to make a relatively small investment in a potentially lucrative ad hoc dispensary model. Realistically, if a source of supply can be secured, setting up a dispensary in Canada is no more expensive than opening any other retail location. If a businessperson is prepared to operate a technically illegal store in the hope that the police and Crown will ignore it, they can usually make money. As there are over 400 ad hoc dispensaries operating in Canada as I write, this would seem to be an attractive business option, other than the now tangible risk of arrest.

Alternatively, a Canadian interested in operating within the law will likely have to wait for some time for the legalizing legislation to be passed by Parliament, and then for the regulations to be written and issued. It will probably be a long wait. In the interim, the ad hoc dispensaries may have saturated the medical and recreational markets, established reputations and branding, and begun the process of driving prices down through competition.

Unless the growing dispensary movement is fairly quickly brought to legal heel, the entire legalization and regulation process in Canada may well be rendered moot because the ad hoc dispensaries will become established, municipally licensed, and politically active. A legal move against the ad hoc dispensaries would require a good deal of political will which, especially in the face of pending federal legalization, does not appear to be present in many jurisdictions but that, as the raids in Toronto demonstrated, can change without warning.

So, for businesspeople, entry into Canada's surprisingly unregulated marijuana market becomes a balance between the desire not to break the law and a realization that the market opportunity of marijuana is being seized by people who do not see the law as having political, prosecutorial, or police support. At the moment Canada's marijuana marketplace is a high risk, high reward "Wild West," and the sheriff seems a long way away.

Branding, Marketing, Advertising, and Location

6

Your branding, marketing, advertising, and location are interconnected and should all be considered carefully.

1. Branding

It may sound obvious but your store is your brand, and your brand will tend to define your store.

A brand is much more than just the look and feel, a logo, or a sign; it is the embodiment of your vision of what your marijuana retail operation is all about. For example, although I have yet to see this done, you may want your pot shop to cater to the budget-minded marijuana consumer. Once you have made that decision, you then can come up with a name for your store: Budget Cannabis? Cheap Thrills? Rock Bottom Pot? Perhaps Naturally High, Premium Organic Cannabis, or Artisan Pot would work for a pot shop all about organic, chemical-free marijuana. What you are looking for is a name which instantly conveys the particular approach you are taking to retailing marijuana.

Deciding what you want your brand to be is critical. The fact is that designers, marketers, architects, and web gurus can only work effectively when they have clear direction from their client: you.

Once you have your own idea for a store brand, it is time to refine that idea before bringing in professionals. If you have a location in mind, take a walk and see how your store might fit into the neighborhood,

or stand out. Go back to your demographic statistics and consider if your branding will hit the sweet spot in the demographic you want to reach. Think carefully about what you see your store's logo looking like and then think about how that will look as a sign for your store or on a website. Most of us are not design whizzes, but a pad of paper, a pencil, and some time can give you a feel for what you want a designer to do.

1.1 Look and feel

In the process of working through your business idea and your business plan, you will encounter many questions and decisions about how your business is going to face the public.

These questions and decisions begin as far back as when you chose a name for your company — if incorporated — and the name of your retail outlet (not necessarily the same). Think of it as branding; It is important to the success of your marijuana retail business whether you are in a maturing, competitive market, or preparing to enter a market where marijuana has only recently been legalized.

Retailers spend millions of dollars developing a look and feel for their operations which will appeal to specific market segments. What works for The Gap is different from what will work for Walmart and on a different planet from Chanel. What works in a small town may not work at all in a city or even a suburb. A pot shop in an urban neighborhood may want very different branding from one in a college town.

The process of coming up with branding and a sense of how your retail marijuana operation will reach its market can generally be described as deciding on a look and feel for that operation.

Whether you are planning a multimillion-dollar, fully integrated, seed to sale, multiple outlet operation, or a little pot shop in a small town, your marijuana retail operation is yours. What do you want it to look like?

There is no right way to create the look and feel of a retail store. If you are planning a medical marijuana dispensary you might have a vision of an old style apothecary with glass jars and rough wood floors. Or you could adopt a pharmacy-driven look with white and chrome fixtures, and staff in lab coats. Pot shops can range from echoes of the head shops of the 1970s all the way through to a gentlemen's cigar shop look or a Restoration Hardware vibe. Or, you can be purely functional and let the product sell itself.

If you don't have a solid idea of what you want your outlet to look like, spend an hour or two online and look at the shops in Washington and Colorado. You'll see a huge range of options. Pick a few you like and make sure you bookmark the pages as you go. If you are in or near one of the states where marijuana has been legalized, it makes sense to take a road trip and see what other people have done. You may not find exactly what you want, but you are sure to find lots of versions of what you don't want. That will narrow the range of choices when it comes to deciding on your vision.

1.2 The design brief

When you have a vision of your retail marijuana business, it is time to write a design brief. This is a document which summarizes what you want from the professionals you are going to bring into the design process. Given the costs involved with opening a store it makes a lot of sense to use professionals for the various design elements. Yes, you can do it yourself and save a few thousand dollars, but unless you are an experienced graphic designer and trained website architect, hiring talent makes more sense. Even the best talent needs direction from the client. A design brief gives them direction.

A good design brief will give the designer and other professionals a summary of your vision for your store, a clear idea of the creative material required: logo, signage, packaging on the graphic end, website, Facebook and other social media on the web, interior design including fixtures, and from the architect side, store renovations. It will also include information on your target market, any demographic information which you have acquired, and possibly a section on competitors in the market.

A design brief which starts with "Cannabis Solutions Inc. will sell premium-grade marijuana in the X district of X" gives a designer a sense of what your business is about.

"Our target market is 30–45-year-old males interested in a more artisanal approach to cannabis. We are targeting a market which is fairly price insensitive but obsessed with quality and authenticity" will give the designer information about where to aim the design. What appeals to women under 30 is not the same as what will appeal to men over 50, though both are market segments a retail marijuana outlet might wish to target (likely not at the same time from the same store).

Including an array of logos and branding from stores which you think are "doing it right" also helps a designer by showing them what you are looking for.

You may include the interior design vision of your store as part of the design brief, or you may want to do a separate brief for a store designer. The statements about what you intend to do and who your target market is will be the same in both briefs but the deliverables will be different.

A design brief may include a budget figure for the various design elements. However, unless you have been through the process before, you are unlikely to have a detailed knowledge of what each of the elements will cost. In those circumstances you may want to give a global budget as well as budgets for the various components which will include logo, signage, packaging, web presence, and store interior design.

If you are a design novice, along with doing some basic research on the Internet, it's worthwhile to pay a graphic designer to walk you through what you need graphically with approximate costs. You can do the same with a web and interior designer. This sort of walkthrough will give you the basic concepts, language, and sense of costs. As with a lawyer or an accountant, a designer is a professional whose time is their only source of income. Paying a few hundred dollars up front can save thousands down the line.

If you are able to "speak the language" you can actually write a request for proposals and get quotes from several designers. This makes sense when there are several thousand dollars involved and can get you a good price but, as important, a sense of which designer "gets" what you actually want.

2. Designers, Architects, and Merchandisers

At the earliest stage of your marijuana retail businesses development you should look around for a lawyer and an accountant; recognize the need for the expertise these professionals will bring to your project. Unfortunately, many start-up retail entrepreneurs are not willing to spend the money to hire excellent designers, architects, and merchandisers. This is almost always a mistake because these professionals will save you money and create branding, a space, and a product range which will make you money.

A good designer works closely with his or her client to come up with a graphic representation of your vision for your brand, your store, and your company. In the design field there is a significant degree of specialization but there is also a degree of overlap. Most graphic designers can deal with logos, packaging, signage, and ads, and some will also be able to create an excellent website. However, graphic designers are usually unwilling to take on interior design projects, or the "copy," or writing end of a project.

Store designers are just that. They figure out the layout of the interior of your store, provide input on such things as window and showcase displays, work out traffic flows, colors, finishes, and all the hundreds of details which make for an appealing retail experience. They understand lighting, which is much more important than you might think. Store designers know where to source the display cabinets, counters, and other fixtures a store needs.

For larger projects where there will be a degree of renovation involved in realizing the vision for your store, the services of an architect can be useful. Architects not only design and plan renovation projects, they also bring a familiarity with the planning and permitting process in the jurisdiction in which you are planning on opening. Architect services are especially valuable where you are planning on changing the use of the space you are going to use as your location. That great gas station in a hip neighborhood may look perfect for your pot shop but changing a building's use can raise a host of municipal issues through which a competent architect can steer you.

One other professional you might think about consulting is a merchandiser. Merchandisers think about how to set up your store to move product. They think about things such as sales, point of sale displays, where to place high margin products, and the visual presentation of your store.

2.1 Target market: Local focus or out of towners

Pot tourism is a real thing. In many jurisdictions marijuana, medicinal or recreational, remains illegal. People will often make a special trip to jurisdictions where smoking their favorite herb does not risk a jail term.

While out of town customers are unlikely to form a large part of a particular pot shop's customer base, a location near tourist districts in your city or town may make sense for certain sorts of marijuana retail operations.

The marijuana tourist trade can tip the balance between two otherwise equivalent locations. While the tourist trade is usually seasonal, having a few months a year of enhanced revenues can make a significant difference to the profitability of your store.

That said, when recreational marijuana was first legalized in Colorado, green tours were organized and stores reported up to 50 percent of their customers were from out of state. Apparently these numbers declined over the years pot has been legal, but out of state purchasers are still a significant part of some stores' business.

3. Creating the Retail Experience

When cannabis is first legalized in a jurisdiction there is something of a Green Rush with sometimes hundreds of stores all opening in a hurry to cash in on the buzz surrounding legal pot. While these stores will likely be compliant with whatever the regulatory scheme requires, only a few of them will have spent the time to consider what sort of retail experience they want their clients to have.

Medical marijuana dispensaries are fortunate because they can have a simple, pharmacy-based design model which is either required by regulation or demanded by municipal bylaws. While such restrictions can be frustrating, they also mean the regulated medical marijuana dispensary owner has fewer and less expensive options than the recreational pot shop proprietor.

However, paying attention to the medical marijuana retail experience can make a dispensary stand out. Simple things such as consistent labeling, good product visibility, and excellent — but not harsh — lighting can make a dispensary a warm, inviting place for its clients.

Depending on the regulatory situation and the advice of your lawyer and accountant on tax implications, setting a dispensary up so that the cannabis itself occupies a very small footprint may allow workarounds for the IRS anti-trafficking deduction rules. As well, where permitted, selling higher margin delivery systems such as vaporizers, glassware, and other cannabis accessories can be a profitable use of space.

While a medical marijuana dispensary can be very functional and somewhat clinical, it can also opt for a more "health food/vitamin shop" look. Some dispensary owners prefer a retail experience where the customer buys the product with a minimum of staff contact. Others will look to create an environment where customers will feel encouraged to discuss and explore their medical marijuana alternatives and consider the best way to take their medicine. Either model can work; but it is important to bear in mind that the margins on medical marijuana are often fairly thin. Enhancing your customer's retail experience is a great idea but it needs to connect to the profitability of your dispensary.

On the recreational side, under most regulatory regimes, there is a great deal more room to enhance your customer's retail experience. There is also far more reason to do so as your store is in direct competition with other recreational pot shops for customers' discretionary dollars.

At the very earliest stages of your planning, a recreational pot shop owner needs to think about the sort of experience a store is going to provide and, more importantly, why that particular experience is desirable and how it will contribute to the profitability of the store.

Having a clear idea of the target market demographic is a good place to start. Old or young, male or female, ethnicity? Oddly, an easy way to get a handle on this is to think seriously about what sort of music would be playing in your store if you a) are allowed to play music, and b) decide you will. In many ways the decision on music — hip hop or EDM, classic rock, country, or New Age — tells you a lot about who you envision your customers to be.

In the regulated recreational market there are certain requirements for marijuana sales. For example, in Colorado there is a distinction between how much pot a resident of the state can buy versus an out-of-state buyer. There are, of course, age rules to follow as well.

Some pot shops have adopted a "check-in desk" approach to dealing with ID issues. Basically, at the front of the shop, there is a station where customers present ID before being allowed into the store. This may seem a bit harsh but it gets the ID issue out of the way and lets your customer shop without further hassles. Other stores are happy to incorporate an ID check as part of the checkout procedure.

The actual sales process can range from a vending machine approach where the customer goes to a machine, makes a choice, and inserts cash, to a quite intensive hand-selling model. How you decide to sell marijuana determines the customer experience you want to create. It also is a huge determinant of your cost of sales. The more customer interaction you have the higher your staffing costs because the last thing you want is a potential customer unable to purchase due to there being no one available to help.

Because of security and regulatory concerns, cannabis products are not usually directly available to the customer. The customer experience will, at minimum, involve asking a salesperson for a particular sort and quantity of marijuana. In a budget environment that may be the sum of the interaction other than payment. In more customer-aware pot shops, salespeople — a.k.a., bud wranglers — offer a good deal of information to the customer. They need to be knowledgeable, friendly, and able to provide a great customer experience quickly when there are lots of customers to serve.

Thinking about issues such as space, traffic flow, and lighting can create an environment where the marijuana is the star and customers get a sense of being taken care of. People who design stores for a living are driven by detail. Simply having great lighting can improve sales per square foot significantly.

3.1 Curb appeal

Regardless of where you locate, if you are doing retail you need to draw customers into your store. Conventionally, stores have signs, show windows, and entrances. A trip to a high-end mall will give you a look at one aesthetic; a trip to a hipster shopping district with microbrew pubs, vintage clothing shops, and vape stores will give you another. And, unfortunately, a close reading of your jurisdiction's marijuana regulations will give you the constraints with which you will have to work. You may also have to deal with municipal regulations which limit design choices.

The regulations can be onerous. In Washington, stores are restricted to one 1,600 square-inch sign and are not permitted to display marijuana products or imagery in their windows. In fact, in some jurisdictions, not only are window displays prohibited but the windows must be opaque so that the marijuana is invisible from the street.

As well as the regulations, there is the issue of security. We discuss this in Chapter 7, but the need for security may require security bars or grates across the windows.

All in all, the combination of regulatory and security requirements can create a pretty forbidding exterior. In particular, mirrored windows and black iron bars combine to make your retail marijuana shop look more like an adult video shop than a welcoming environment.

A bit of creativity can turn a blank window into an intriguing, open space. Even if you can't use your windows to sell pot, you can use them for things like displaying art or sculpture. Or, you can set up interesting lighting which changes hour to hour. Doing something witty like displaying a single, really well lit bag of Doritos dead center in the window can convey a message.

The point being that the less like a fortress and more like a normal retail store you can make the exterior of your pot shop, the better.

At the same time, good, old-fashioned Chamber of Commerce virtues are surprisingly useful. Strange as it may sound, sweeping the sidewalk in front of your store tends to increase sales. So do grace notes like flower pots or ornamental trees. Cleaning your windows (even if they are opaque) weekly and removing graffitti immediately will tend to make your store more inviting.

If you have a standalone store it makes sense to think about things like parking and landscaping. Again, the old-fashioned approach of keeping your parking lot spotless and your landscaping taken care of will create a sense that you care about the environment in which you are working.

There is never a reason not to have your storefront freshly painted and things like your door hardware gleaming. Also, test your door before you open: Customers should not have to fight with your door. Having a mat on the floor as the customers come in gives them a chance to shake the rain off. Having excellent lighting over your door and, if you can afford it, right across your storefront, will make your pot shop a welcoming place on a dark night.

If you are in a less restrictive jurisdiction, you obviously have more choices on how to intrigue your customers. You may not be allowed to display the cannabis or cannabis products but you may be able to put glassware, vaporizers, and other attractive paraphernalia in the window. Window display is an art in itself and can range from a maximal, "more is more" approach to Zen-like simplicity with a single object the focus of brilliant lighting.

It is also important to look at the stores around you; not because you have to blend in but because they reflect their years of retail experience in your particular neighborhood.

Your store will have signage of some sort. In your design process, along with regulatory concerns, it is a good idea to look at your location and the sorts of signs which surround you. What works in a strip mall will fail on a standalone store and be out of place in a higher end retail location. Signs can be surprisingly expensive and getting it right the first time is a huge plus.

Letting people know you are open does not have to involve a red LED or neon "open" sign. It can, but it is often a better idea to have an attractive, easy-to-read, well-lit, painted sign.

Curb appeal — enticing customers — is often all about small details. Looking clean and up-to-date is always more attractive than appearing run down and as if you've seen better days.

4. Location

Speaking of all this curb appeal and retail brilliance, where is it going to be?

Take a moment to think about the purchase decision of a marijuana user. When marijuana is first legalized in a jurisdiction, the sheer novelty of being able to buy pot legally drives initial sales. However, the novelty soon wears off. Now, more run of the mill purchase decisions are made. The most common triggers for the decision are that a customer is running low on pot, has run out of pot, or has been out of pot for some time but only now has the money to buy more pot. Yes, there will be customers who want to try a different variety of pot or a different delivery system, but the majority of your customers will likely already have particular preferences.

When people talk about the location of a business they pack a lot of assumptions into the idea. Like high foot traffic being important, parking matters, and the demographics of the neighborhood can predict success or failure. There are also assumptions about the effect of having competitors nearby and public transit or freeway access. Consultants make good livings comparing and contrasting various locations for retail businesses.

Location is also constrained by the marijuana regulations in your jurisdiction, municipal bylaws, prohibitions against marijuana businesses adopted by certain landlords, the general commercial space market in your locality and, of course, what you can afford. Plus, depending on your jurisdiction's regulations, you may require space which can be physically separated so as to set the actual marijuana out of reach. Finally, you need to consider the security of your retail operation. There is no one size fits all, right answer to the location question. Instead there are sets of business considerations which, if you take them seriously, will let you determine the right location for your marijuana retail business. As always, your location decision should be based on minimizing business risk while maximizing reward.

4.1 Foot traffic, destination stores, clustering

If the vast majority of marijuana purchase decisions are made because potential customers are out of pot, it is likely that they will go out to the pot store to make their purchase. In effect, "the pot store" is a destination.

If the majority of your customers are destination-driven in principle, as long as your store is relatively close to major traffic routes and public transit, it makes very little difference if it is on a busy pedestrian street or tucked away in a corner largely invisible to the public, but it will make a huge difference to your store's bottom line. Low foot traffic, low visibility locations are leased at a small fraction of the cost of locations in busy retail areas.

Lower traffic areas offer other advantages if your customers are destination driven. First, because the lease rate will be lower, you can afford larger premises. Leaving aside situations in which you are actually growing your product and therefore need a significant quantity of non-retail space, having more space allows you to display more product. Given the proliferation of marijuana products — edibles alone offer literally thousands of products — if you want your store to sell across many categories you will need that space.

Extra space also allows display and sale of high-margin, non-regulated items such as glassware and vaporizers, where permitted. It may also allow a marijuana retailer to physically divide the premises into medical and recreational sections (where permitted) and, with the advice of counsel, may allow operations classified as trafficking by the IRS to be isolated from the main premises which may result in significant tax savings. Ample space can also facilitate a check-in area where ID can be checked prior to entry.

As well as extra space, a destination approach allows a store to be located where there is ample parking and low traffic congestion.

The other side of the argument is that placing your store in a high-traffic area will push your brand simply because of your visibility of your store. And, where permitted, clusters of marijuana stores can become destinations in themselves as demonstrated by Denver's famous Green Mile.

The clustering effect does not have to be limited to marijuana stores. Opening a recreational pot shop in a cluster of stores catering to a specific, pot friendly demographic makes sense. If your target market is neo-boho youth skewed, you could do worse than locating near a cluster of vintage clothing, vinyl record, and vape stores, across the street from a microbrewery.

Going for high visibility, high-traffic locations means higher lease rates and, usually, a smaller store footprint with a correspondingly smaller selection of goods. This can work well if the margins on those goods is high. Hitting a market sweet spot, while it is challenging, can be very lucrative.

Regardless of whether you see your marijuana retail operation as a destination store or driven by foot traffic, it is important to examine the demographics of the area you are considering. A large number of college students within a one mile circle of your proposed location might be ideal for your sort of pot shop. Or you might want to reach out to an older demographic with a health and well-being approach, in which case you need to take a serious look at the demographic information you gathered for your business plan to identify ideal locations. If an older, wellness-driven client base is your target, look for a Whole Foods-type of store and you won't go far wrong.

4.2 Zoning and legal issues

Depending on your jurisdiction, there will likely be regulations which prohibit the location of a medical marijuana dispensary or recreational pot shop within a set distance of buildings such as schools, parks, churches, and, in some cases, other marijuana-selling operations.

It is important to know the rules before you even think about leasing a space. In particular, not only do you need to know the distance required as set out in the regulations, you also need to know how that distance is measured. A 1,000 foot as the crow flies exclusion zone is very different from a walking distance zone, and both are difficult to measure on Google Maps.

Does your area have rules governing medical marijuana dispensaries and pot shops? In Colorado, for example, many have used their power to ban recreational pot shops despite the state-wide legalization of recreational pot.

There are also specific zoning by-laws which prohibit certain uses for land zoned for other uses. A retail store operation may be prohibited in a building on land zoned light industrial. In general, changing the zoning on a particular building is difficult, time consuming, and expensive. However, if you find the ideal location but the zoning is wrong, it may be worth checking with a municipal lawyer as to whether a zoning change or exemption might be possible.

As well as zoning issues, there are also often municipal bylaws which govern change of use of a building even where the zoning permits such a use. Change of use applications tend to be more routine that zoning issues but the help of an architect is often critical to success.

If you find a great location and a space which could work with some renovation. it is a very good idea to check the rules in your municipality regarding such renovations. You will probably need a building permit for anything significant and typically that is easy to get. However, you may find that even a minor renovation triggers a set of new requirements which have little to do with your project. Requirements such as wheelchair accessibility, washroom facilities for people with disabilities, modernizing fire protection, and even seismic upgrading can add huge costs to what initially appeared to be a small project.

A final wrinkle may be parking requirements and restrictions. Some municipalities require onsite parking for customers and/or employees. A space you might be considering for a storage area or extension may, in fact, be seen as parking by your municipality.

Along with all of these considerations, every location comes with a set of rules regarding things like signage, sidewalk signs, and sometimes even design rules which prevent you from substantially changing a heritage exterior.

The old expression, "You can't fight City Hall" is just as much a reality for a marijuana retail outlet as it is for any other store. Various legal requirements and restrictions can add large and sometimes unpredictable costs. You can reduce those costs and the uncertainty which can surround them by looking for a space which is very close to what you need. A location which was formerly a retail store will already have the zoning and permitted use baked in. You may not love the layout of the space but, if it is in the right location, the interior layout can often be changed without having to undertake renovations and therefore getting a building permit.

4.3 Neighborhoods and districts

Whether you see your retail store as a destination location or driven by foot traffic, your retail outlet will be in some sort of neighborhood or district.

The whole idea of neighborhood is difficult to define. However, people quite easily talk about "X" being a good neighborhood and "Y" being a tough part of town. In suburbs there will be upscale malls and shopping streets and there will be more middle-of-the-road streets and malls. Clusters of big-box stores will draw traffic but by no stretch of the imagination can be thought of as neighborhoods. And not every stretch of housing and shopping streets becomes a neighborhood.

When you are considering possible locations, the idea of neighborhood or district is important. You would ideally like to find a neighborhood where your marijuana store will be welcome, but you also need to find a neighborhood where you can afford the rent.

Getting the positives — foot traffic, parking, demographics — exactly right may be next to impossible; but to minimize your risk you need to make sure you avoid the negatives. Negatives for a neighborhood are things like street crime, run-down storefronts, vacant lots, lack of secure parking, and incompatible businesses. There is a difference between an edgy, gentrifying neighborhood and one where derelict buildings house failing businesses.

Neighborhoods often have sharp boundaries. You may think a storefront is in a hip, trending neighborhood when, in fact, it is a couple of blocks away from the sweet spot and might as well be in a different city. The only way to figure out things like boundaries is to spend time there. Go during business hours on weekdays and weekends. Look at the people in the neighborhood. If you have a clear idea of who your ideal customer is, see if you spot many of them. It is subjective and unscientific, but using your eyes and chatting with shopkeepers and servers will let you ground truth a potential location.

4.4 Commercial real estate agents

As you walk through a neighborhood in which you are thinking of locating you are likely to see real estate signs offering premises for lease. Many will have the name of an agent on them. Take notes.

Commercial real estate is a very different business from residential. First off, most of the transactions are for commercial leases rather than the outright sale of premises. Second, commercial real estate has very different terms and conditions from either a house sale or a residential tenancy. Third, in many cities only a small fraction of the available commercial space is advertised as being for lease. Fourth, for a commercial landlord, a lease is seen as an asset, the value of which is usually negotiable.

The attractive storefront you see in a busy neighborhood will likely be owned by a commercial landlord as part of a set of commercial real estate holdings. The landlord's objective is to find a suitable tenant who will sign a lease running for several years at a base rent plus property taxes, building insurance, and common area maintenance (known as a triple net lease). The landlord wants a solvent tenant, which means credit checks on both the company and its owner, and will often want a personal guarantee. For the right tenant, the landlord may offer reduced or waived base rent for a period of months at the beginning of the lease, an escalating base rent with low payments in the first years of a multi-year lease, and, in some cases, leasehold improvements — things like walls and washrooms as well as some fixtures — as inducements to the tenant. There are, in fact, no fixed terms in a commercial lease and everything is potentially negotiable.

This is where a good commercial real estate agent can be invaluable. Most businesspeople know next to nothing about commercial leasing. Most store owners only have one or, at most, three or four locations so they are not dealing with commercial leases very often. As well, many businesspeople know next to nothing about the state of the commercial real estate market.

Commercial real estate agents know the market, often have access to useful information such as area traffic counts, and have day-to-day knowledge of what sorts of deals are being done in your city and in your chosen neighborhood. They understand the terms which go into commercial leasing agreements.

Simply understanding the hidden costs in a triple net lease, spotting excessive common area fees or high insurance costs, can save a tenant significant money over a five year lease. Being familiar with comparatives in the city will level the negotiating playing field. Having a good commercial real estate broker can give you a valuable edge as you walk into a negotiation which may determine the long run success or failure of your business.

For a tenant, the best part of hiring a commercial real estate agent is that the agent's commission is usually priced into the lease rate so your landlord will pay your agent. You will get the benefit of the advice of your commercial real estate agent free.

4.5 Commercial leases, closing dates, and lawyers

When the negotiations have concluded and your commercial real estate agent has gotten you the best deal possible, that deal will be written up into a commercial agreement by, in almost every case, the landlord's lawyer. That lawyer will be working from documentation of the negotiated terms — often a much modified Offer to Lease containing the relevant business items — plus what most landlords will maintain is their standard lease. An Offer to Lease generally sets out the key business terms, including the legal names of the parties; a description of the premises (usually with measurements); the rent; other payments (taxes, insurance, and maintenance); term and commencement date; renewal options; tenant inducements; effect of sale of the building or sale of the business; and any pre-conditions for the benefit of either party.

Even a simple commercial lease, negotiated with the advice of a competent commercial real estate agent, can be a bit of a nightmare. In particular, many tenants are more than a little surprised to discover the Offer to Lease is, in fact, a binding agreement. Key point: Have your lawyer review the Offer to Lease document carefully before you sign.

Your lawyer in this case may or may not be the lawyer you are using to navigate your way through the marijuana licensing process. Regulatory law is very different from real estate law and if there is any complexity at all to your arrangement for leasing your location it is usually worth the money to hire a specialist. Your commercial real estate agent will have worked with a variety of real estate lawyers and will likely have recommendations.

In the process of negotiating a commercial lease there will usually be a designated date for closing the transaction. On that date you will take formal possession of the premises and the rent and other costs will be payable going forward. This may not be the formal occupancy date. Where there are leasehold improvements being undertaken by the landlord there may be some time between the closing date and your occupancy. In many cases rent and costs may be waived for the period between closing and occupancy but only if that term is included in the Offer to Lease.

At closing you may be signing the formal lease or you may be signing the final version of the Offer to Lease which usually contains a requirement to sign the formal lease. There may also be documents which give a form of your personal guarantee that you will pay personally what is owed under the lease. You should know before you go in what you will be signing and your lawyer should have seen and approved every document you are going to sign. Usually, you will be accompanied by your agent to the closing. On larger closings your lawyer may come as well, but at several hundred dollars an hour, that may be a luxury with which you can dispense.

At closing, there will be an agreed amount of money you will pay to the landlord. Even where you have negotiated "free" rent for several months, such a concession rarely applies to the taxes, insurance, and maintenance. There may, as well, be other fees to be paid at closing. Some landlords will insist on a certified check for the full amount, others will take a company check or a check from your lawyer's trust account. No matter what, make sure that check is covered.

4.6 Security

Security is important enough to warrant its own chapter (Chapter 7). However, security issues are significant when choosing a location.

First, there are regulatory security obligations: rules going to video surveillance, cash and product tracking, and the physical security of the store and, if you have one, the growing operation.

Second, there are your own security concerns. Issues such as whether your location can be secured overnight and if there is space for a safe, a safe room, and secure product storage. Is there space for secure loading and unloading of product and cash?

Third, there are the security concerns posed by the neighborhood. How safe is the neighborhood; is there safe parking for staff and customers? What sort of neighbors does your proposed location have? Are there good street lights? Is there a homelessness or gang problem in the neighborhood?

Some potential locations are inherently more secure than others. Some locations can be made secure with an investment in changes to the interior or exterior of the building. These are questions which you need to address before even thinking about making an Offer to Lease.

When considering security issues it is important to remember that your landlord will have to approve significant alterations to the interior or exterior of the premises you are renting. A security plan which calls for a fence or a wall to be built to improve the security of the rear area of a building may not be permitted by the landlord (or the municipality for that matter).

Once you have narrowed your location search to a couple of possibilities, it makes sense to have a security consultant walk through the premises and assess suitability. What looks to you like a perfect location may have irremediable security problems you need to know about before you make a binding offer to lease.

Where a security professional suggests changes, these need to be, at a minimum, outlined for the landlord's approval in the Offer to Lease. However, they can also be included as leasehold improvements which the landlord pays for as part of the "tenant inducement package" most long term leases include. You'll end up paying for them in the end through the rent; but at start-up, when cash is tight, having often expensive security renovations paid for by your landlord is very good for your cash flow.

5. Advertising, The Internet, and Location

What if you cannot find or cannot afford what you think is the ideal location for your dispensary or pot shop?

A less-than-perfect location can sometimes be overcome with clever advertising. However, conventional advertising can be expensive. Also, because of the regulated nature of the marijuana market, there are fairly strict rules on advertising in many of the places where marijuana has been legalized. Even bumper stickers advertising pot ships are forbidden in Washington State on the basis that the cars they are attached to might be driven within 1,000 feet of a school.

The Internet offers alternatives to conventional print or television advertising, beginning with a retail marijuana store's website. A good website, with clear directions to your store, a good map, information about products for sale, and whatever else makes sense, that stays within the regulations can put your store top of mind for nearby cannabis users.

However, a website is just the beginning. A useful Facebook page, a Twitter account, and a pot blog are all bits of social media which can bring in customers. Developing a solid internet strategy and understanding ideas like Search Engine Optimization (SEO) and localization can improve even a bad location's visibility where it matters.

Where it matters most is on people's smartphones. You need a website which is responsive, meaning it automatically adapts to the device upon which it is viewed. You may also need an app for your store although, realistically, getting widespread adoption of your store's app is a marketing challenge in itself. There are apps designed to bring information about recreational and medical retail stores to cannabis users. Leafy and WeedMaps are two go-to apps for users. Making sure that your store is on Yelp and on Google Maps, and encouraging your customers to review your products and services can improve your visibility where it counts.

From a business risk perspective, where a high rent is a monthly burden, a well-thought-out and implemented web and smartphone strategy can be a fairly contained upfront cost and a low monthly upkeep cost. The idea of an ideal location changes a lot if it turns out that most of your customers first find you using their phone.

6. Marketing

The happy idea that you open your doors for business and the world walks in is never true. Certainly, when a marijuana shop opens in a jurisdiction where it has just been legalized, there will be an initial rush of curious customers, but that rush dwindles. Which means that every recreational marijuana shop and medical marijuana dispensary needs a marketing strategy and it needs it long before the shop is open.

You have been building your marketing strategy from the moment you decided to go into the marijuana business. The demographic factors you considered when choosing a location were about marketing; the choice of products to offer and prices to charge were marketing; so were the design decisions you made about your storefront, signage, displays, and packaging. Marketing drives every decision a store owner makes even if the store owner is not really aware of that fact.

Marketing is what brings people to your store the first time and what brings them back over and over. That fact gives a marijuana store owner a handle on the marketing function because it is broad enough to cover the many activities which add up to a marketing strategy.

Even a store which does no advertising, appears on no websites, and has generic signage and packaging is adopting a marketing strategy: word of mouth. This is a strategy which, depending on circumstances, can be very successful. However, word of mouth is a strategy which, by default, every store and every marijuana store adopts. The question is how you can go further.

6.1 A word on costs and ROI

Setting up a marijuana store, stocking it with products, setting up security cameras and safe rooms, and putting in fixtures and point of sales systems are all going to cost money. So will rent, salaries and wages, insurance, ongoing security coverage, cash management solutions, and so on. These are costs over which you have very little control. Your accountant will explain it all in terms of fixed and variable costs but a more colloquial way of putting it is that these costs are your monthly "nut"; what it takes to keep your stores open.

Another set of costs are discretionary. You can choose how much to spend. Some of these are internal; for example hiring an extra staffer for your busy times to improve customer experience and let you sell more product. Some are external. All marketing costs, advertising, web presence, public relations, and store-branded merchandise are discretionary and external costs. You don't have to spend any money on marketing, but it is usually a good idea to develop a marketing plan and budget.

Critically, marketing needs to pay its way. Your accountant will talk about Return on Investment (ROI), and it is a very useful concept. If you spend $100 on an advertisement, what are your expectations about how much business that will generate and what actual return will it bring you? Remember you need to calculate that return based on the cost of the action, the increase in sales it generates less your fixed costs and the cost of goods sold. In other words, if your $100 ad creates $150 in new business, your return after fixed costs and cost of goods sold might only be a net few dollars.

There are a lot of free or very low-cost marketing strategies which will increase the volume of your business without much cash outlay. As a general rule you should make sure you are doing the low cost things well before you spend precious dollars on advertising or other marketing options. The ROI on free is, by definition, pretty much infinite.

6.2 Being found

To buy from your store, people have to be able to find it, and they have to have some idea what you are selling. It seems obvious but it is surprising how many marijuana dispensaries and retail locations have lovely but deeply mysterious names. Nature's Bounty, Celestial Healing, Elevation, or Twist may be wonderful words and phrases but, unless they have a subtitle, a potential customer has no idea what they are selling. Simply choosing a name with "marijuana" or "cannabis" or "weed" in it makes it obvious.

Paying attention to your signage and window displays (where permitted) will let passersby know what you are selling as well. Don't make your potential customers guess.

Simple things, like having your address and your website on everything from advertising to packaging to sales receipts, gives people your coordinates. Making sure your graphic designer understands that nothing goes to print without your address is a simple, cheap bit of marketing.

While marketers will talk about building a brand, and that may be important for your marijuana store, the fact is that taking care of the simple issue of where to find your store is, when you are first open, more important.

Similarly, if you are allowed to advertise and have a budget, your initial advertising buys should be all about location. While you may want to start advertising your special strains and blends or your incredible edibles, you need to make sure that your location is front and center in your early advertising.

6.3 Market segmentation and targeting

If you are located in a larger urban area you might have a few hundred thousand people within a 20-minute drive from your store. However, of that population only a relatively small percentage will be interested in your marijuana products. Who are they? How do you reach them?

A huge part of a well-planned marketing strategy is to understand who you wish to reach with your marketing efforts. For example, if you are a medical marijuana dispensary your target markets will be significantly different from the target markets of the recreational pot shop down the block.

If you made a business plan you have done some basic market analysis. You have done the research on who buys marijuana. So has the State of Colorado. In 2014 it published a report called "Market Size and Demand for Marijuana in Colorado" (see download kit for a link to it). While it does not do demographic breakdowns of marijuana users, it provides evidence that heavy users drive demand for recreational pot. This may seem obvious but the numbers are striking with 20 percent of users creating 80 percent of sales.

The State of Colorado has also provided a helpful infographic on some demographic characteristics of marijuana users in that state, and a link to it is available on the download kit as well.

These are potential starting points for your own analysis. However, the fact that marijuana use is highest in lower income groups or among the less educated does not mean your store needs to focus on these target demographics. Rather it suggests that it will take well-focused marketing to reach other demographics.

6.4 The web

Every marijuana retail store needs to bake the Internet into its marketing strategy. However, the Internet is a big place with a lot of options and, because of license restrictions, you may be limited as to what you can put on the web. Plus, just because you have a website does not mean anyone will be able to find your website. Finally, third-party websites and searches may turn out to be more important for your business than your website itself.

Any web strategy you adopt should be driven by your overall marketing plan and be part of your marketing budget.

A few basic things you need to do well before you open your store:

Get a domain name: this seems obvious until you think about the effect a domain name has on various search engines. Having your specific location as part of your domain name may help you get great Google rankings in your city. Or you can have a main website with your store name and a few other domain names which are location specific and are linked or redirected to your main site.

- **Register social media accounts:** Use Facebook and Twitter at a minimum but you may want to look at Pinterest, Instagram, and SnapChat.

- **Register for Google business:** This is a key move because Google Business is the gateway into things like Google Maps and Google local business listings.

- **Develop a review strategy:** Google Reviews, Yelp, and Yellow Pages all cover recreational marijuana stores and dispensaries. Google Reviews can appear at the top of searches for marijuana stores in your area. Being reviewed, and well reviewed, is critical.

- **Identify influential marijuana sites:** As I write, sites like Leafy.com and WeedMaps.com provide locations, reviews and information about recreational and medicinal marijuana stores. There are dozens of other sites competing in this space. Which of these sites will matter to your business is part of the marketing plan. To a degree, different sites appeal to different market segments with some focused on medical marijuana, others on recreational pot. Look for sites which seem to line up with your market focus and then get in touch with the sites which will matter to you and get information about listings and advertising. (This is actually something which is useful to do at the business plan stage.)

- **Understand the basics of search engine position:** When someone Googles "pot in Spokane" they get a set of search engine results. If you are a pot shop in Spokane you want to be on the first page of those results either directly or through a listing or review on a third party site. How you get on that first page of results is a matter of Search Engine Optimization (SEO), localization, reviews, and third party coverage.

  Simple things like great content, links from local businesses, registration with Google Business, and a reviewing and social media strategy all add up to a potential Page One listing. In a fairly small place like Spokane, reaching page one may not be terrifically complicated. For a larger market, like Seattle, the competition for the first page is intense. If your marketing plan is heavily reliant on the Internet, long before you open your store, you need to have a SEO strategy and likely a SEO consultant working to put your shop on Google's front page for the searches you believe are going to bring you customers.

- **Content:** Having a great, static website is pretty much useless in the dynamic world of the Internet. Google's little spiders are voracious and a site which is not updated regularly will fall in the rankings very quickly. Developing a content strategy, likely by way of a blog which automatically updates your social media, is not difficult but it requires commitment. Covering in-store events — sales, new strains, new edibles — is a good first step. Then stepping out and covering information your customers and prospective customers may want lets you keep your site fresh.

Be very careful of "duplicate content." It is all too easy on the Internet to cut and paste a story from another site. Even with full attribution this can hurt you in the Google Page Rank race because Google will see such content as not useful due to duplication.

Backlinks: In simple terms (and with a lot of exceptions) a significant part of a site's Google rank is determined by how many other sites link to it and what authority those sites have. But authority is a funny thing. There are certainly marijuana sites which have tremendous authority and getting even a listing link from one of these sites matters. But there are also sites which have authority for your location. Remember, as a retailer you do not need to have the number one marijuana site in the world, but you do need to be in the top ten for your city and, at an even more granular level, your neighborhood. A local business association or your city government may have more authority for that position than a top pot site. So look for links from local sites as well as the big beasts of the marijuana world.

When you are looking for links it does not hurt to ask for a particular set of words (known as anchor text) to be included in the link. Anchor text is no longer as important as it once was but it certainly does not hurt. For example "Bob's Pot Shop" is not as good as "Bob's Spokane Pot Shop."

Keywords: Consider what searches your customers will actually make. "Marijuana in Spokane" as a search string might be the most common but what about "pot in Spokane" or "weed" or "cannabis"? Google has some brilliant tools in its AdWords offering which lets you check the number of searches for particular keywords. In two minutes I discovered that "marijuana in Spokane" is searched an average of 40 times a month whereas "pot in Spokane" has a mere 10 searches a month.

Using the right keywords in your backlinks and social media can have a great effect on the number of people who find your site.

Consider visitor behavior on your site: Once someone finds your website what do they do? What can they do? Much of the time you will be happy if visitors to your site grab your address and head down to your store. But can you incentivize them? And are such incentives worth it?

Of course you have to check the regulations in your jurisdiction to make sure web incentives are legal but, if they are, you can offer all sorts of web-only discounts and promotions. One store in Seattle offers a $50 Lyft car certificate which you can only get online that is redeemable with purchase at their store.

6.5 Apps and phones

If this book were written in 2006 there would be nothing more to say about online presence. However, these days smartphones and apps for smartphones are a huge part of the online picture. You can get the details in the 2015 Pew Study (link on the download kit), but the takeaways are:

- Sixty-four percent of Americans own a smartphone.

- Fifteen percent of young Americans use smartphones as their primary online access point.

- Seven percent of Americans have no other means of getting online.

- Lower income Americans (a key demographic for recreational pot) are smartphone dependent.

These numbers all suggest that smartphones are a key component to any online marketing strategy.

There are two basic elements to a smartphone-aware online strategy. First, your website must render properly on a smartphone. It is vital for the success of your online marketing program. Second, pay even more attention to localizing your web presence.

Smartphones allow their users to speak their searches. On my Android phone I can say, "OK Google, marijuana in Spokane" and a results page comes up. You want your Spokane marijuana store to come up at the top of that page. The basic Google search, if there is a location mentioned, will give results for that location. A spoken search will get those results. Better still, if you are registered as a Google Business listing, there is every chance that you will be at the top of that page and on the Google map. Localization can be very specific.

Smartphones have bred apps which are single-purpose programs which provide a particular functionality to the smartphone. In particular, there are apps dedicated to locating marijuana stores and dispensaries. Some are geographically aware and will tell the user where the nearest marijuana store is.

Three years ago, say 2013, apps were a very big thing and spending the time and money to be listed on marijuana apps made sense for medical marijuana dispensaries in many states. Now the direct search function on smartphones in combination with the Google localization features make apps less critical. However, a listing on Leafy.com and WeedMaps.com might make sense for a new store simply to build a profile.

(At one point, a few years ago, retail stores saw value in having their own apps created. However, many of those apps, which were often expensive to create, saw very little use and virtually no return. Given limited marketing dollars, creating an app for your store is not likely to have a very high ROI.)

6.6 Push marketing

If you are allowed to do so under the regulations in your jurisdiction, getting the name, email, and cell number of your clients can be exceptionally valuable. Whether through a customer loyalty program, a newsletter, or a strain of the month club, having the contact details of your customers (and their permission) lets you market to people who have already purchased from you.

The value of this information depends on how you use it but if you are able to push a weekly loyalty program special out to, say, 500 smartphones, you will likely sell more product. You can measure the effectiveness of the campaign simply by tracking the sales of that special.

A regular email newsletter will keep your store top of mind for your clients. It does not have to be long, but the newsletter can introduce new products, offer specials, and promote things like the loyalty program or a refer-a-friend campaign.

The value of a good client list is also reflected in the value of the intangibles of your business if you ever plan to sell. If you have been building your list from the day you opened for business, in a few years you will have a list which may represent a couple of hundred thousand dollars in real value to a prospective purchaser.

Permission-based push marketing may turn out to be the secret sauce which makes your retail marijuana store significantly more profitable than that of your competitor down the street. Making the effort to get your clients' permission to reach out to them may, in fact, be the difference between long-term success and failure. It is that important.

7. Local Marketing, Advertising, and Public Relations

A single location marijuana retail store is dependent upon its local community for its customers. Yes, there will be some out of towners, but your bread and butter customers will likely live within a few miles of the store. Reaching out to those customers is the essence of marketing.

Paid advertising can be very effective, where it is permitted. However, free media is even more effective and, well, free.

As ever, you need to be aware of the advertising regulations which govern marijuana licensees in your jurisdiction. Before you plan any advertising or other paid marketing effort, make sure you are allowed to do what you are planning. Because your license is potentially at risk, you do not want to do something which you think is not forbidden by regulation, rather you should try to find things which are expressly permitted. Let your competitors innovate and enjoy the legal headaches which go along with innovation.

8. The Power of the Press Release

Short, to the point, email press releases directed at local media — print and broadcast, as well as web — are inexpensive and can be surprisingly effective. But you have to make the journalists' lives easy. Begin with a snappy headline: "Local Pot Shop Licensed" or "Marijuana Dispensary Opening March 7" or "Bob's Marijuana Store Introduces Pot Brownies." Your headline is also your email subject line, and you want your email opened.

Write your press release as objectively as you can. You do not want to sound promotional, you want to sound factual and you want your journalist target to see a news value in what you have sent. Keep it short. A couple of hundred words at most.

Critically, at the bottom of the press release put in your contact details: Phone and email.

Those are the basics. But a good press release needs someone to read it.

8.1 Know your journalist

Building a short media list — the news editors of the local paper and local alternative paper, the radio and TV news editors, and any local bloggers of interest — is a first step towards a successful public relations campaign. The second step is getting to know who actually writes the sorts of news stories you would like about your shop. This is not difficult with print as many of those stories will carry bylines with the journalists' names and often email addresses. Radio and television is a bit more difficult because there are no bylines. But listen and watch and you'll get the names of the on-air talent.

To get good coverage you need to be more than an emailed press release that comes in once in a while. You need to get to know the journalists who cover your business and the politics which surround it. Perhaps the best way to reach a journalist is to pick up the phone and ask for twenty minutes of their time. If you get that time great, if not they will at least have spoken to you on the phone. A win either way.

Understand that journalism, print or electronic, is a job. Everyday a journalist has to find a story to write about or cover. Some days there is lots of news, other days it is really slow. For the most part the sorts of stories you want to have written about your marijuana retail outlet are not "in the news"; rather they are general interest stories.

If you get 20 minutes with your journalist you can get the conversation started by asking what he or she looks for in a general interest story. What sort of press release will get them to follow up? Most journalists are happy to be asked and usually have a fair bit of useful information to share. Even if they don't, your meeting will have put your store in front of them and made it easier for you to call when you have a story you think might interest them.

Find out about the journalist's interest. Does he or she have a Twitter feed? A blog? If so, follow. What is his or her view on legal marijuana? Does he or she partake? You are trying to establish a connection at a personal level so be interested in what this person has to say.

Do this before you have your store open because when you open, you are going to want to invite the journalists you have connected with for a pre-opening tour of your premises and, if you are having an opening event, to that event.

Great public relations is about relationships. Sending a press release "cold" may occasionally work, but sending a press release with a personal note and a follow-up phone call will produce much better results.

Understand that journalism is competitive to a degree but that it is also a "pack" game where if one journalist is interested in a story others will follow. You won't connect with every journalist on your list but if you are able to reach a few you will begin to get press coverage.

9. A Good Advertisement

Advertising comes in two essential varieties: branding and offers. A branding ad is designed to get your store's name in front of the public with a concise brand message. A logo, a tag line, and your coordinates — address, website, email, and phone — can be all you need. Make sure you have a great name for your store, a brilliant logo, and a really catchy tag line which will score with your target market. If you are aiming at hipster/pot connoisseurs your tag line needs to appeal to that sensibility. If you are going for stoners, a different tag line is needed.

Branding or positioning advertising can be effective, but it is difficult to measure that effectiveness. A good branding ad will put your store top of mind for your target market if they see it. If you put a branding ad online you can at least track the traffic it brings to your site. If you put that same ad in print media you have no effective way to tell if it worked.

Offer ads — where legal — are much easier to track. Essentially an offer ad gives people pricing information, often a sale, about a particular product. You can measure offer ads' effectiveness by how many people come to your store and take the offer.

Advertising operates at two levels: the single ad and the ad campaign. An advertising campaign will tend to have multiple ads on multiple platforms all driving a key message. Generally, all of the ads in a campaign will have the same look and feel, although the advertising copy (the words) and the art may change from ad to ad. An advertising campaign is a commitment and can be fairly expensive. However, by driving a key message, a campaign can put a store top of mind for much of its target market.

Single ads can also be effective but will tend to be less effective as brand ads rather than offer ads. If you take the back page of a small literary magazine with a clever single ad, your brand may be enhanced but it is not obvious that anyone will see the ad. A regular eighth of a page in your local newspaper or alt newspaper with a weekly set of specials will likely produce a greater response. Most print and broadcast media have extensive demographic and psychographic data on their readers/viewers/listeners. It will be in their media kit.

At this point, a word about ad agencies: A good advertising agency can make your journey through paid advertising painless. But at a cost. Agencies usually use a percentage of "ad buy" system. If you spend $10,000 they will want between 20–30 percent of your spend, for which they will do the campaign design and place the ads. You can certainly dicker and it is worth remembering that agencies often take 20 percent from the media in which they place the ads.

The problem with ad agencies is that for a small single outlet marijuana store the advertising budget involved is not likely to attract the larger (and generally better) agencies. If your business and marketing plan calls for a $100,000 one-year budget an agency may make sense, but that sort of money rarely ads up for a marijuana retail location. The alternative is to find a young, creative, smart agency which will see your account as worthwhile in itself and worth nurturing in hopes of an increased ad spend. Ideally, you'll be able to find a young, hungry agency which will give you brilliant creative and a stunning deal. Otherwise, chances are you will have to do it yourself.

9.1 Have a story

Whether you opt for a full-on advertising buy through an ad agency and a contracted PR firm or decide to do it yourself, you have to have a story. From tag lines to full press releases, people want to hear your story; why you are in the marijuana business, how you see marijuana in its culture and our culture.

We tend to see stories as uplifting. In fact they don't need to be. A story about wanting to deliver high THC pot at the lowest possible price will make just as much sense as a story about carefully cured, bio-energetic pot. The point is the narrative; the reason you are the pot business.

For medical marijuana dispensaries the story is usually about the healing achieved by cannabis. These are stories of people who find relief in marijuana. They are stories about the beneficial effects of marijuana. And they are stories about differing ways of delivering the positive effects of cannabis. Most of all they are stories about how the dispensary is in service to its clients.

On the recreational side the stories are quite different. Here you are talking about relaxation, about just how particular strains produce particular states of consciousness. On the recreational side there is a strange reticence. The truth is that people who smoke pot recreationally smoke it to get stoned. Couch locked. Baked. But there is a huge reluctance to actually talk about that. (Which is no different from the liquor stores not talking about the alcohol content of their products and those implications as a selling point.)

Recreational pot stories tend to shy away from the effects of the product and talk about purity, organic production methods, and THC. Telling a story is all about hitting the high points of what you are up to. As the owner of a marijuana retail store you need to think about why you are there and what you want your customers to understand about your business. If you are all about the party then it makes sense for your story to talk about that.

Stories are how stores become landmarks, the place to be; telling your story matters a lot.

9.2 A not very well-kept secret about advertising and its negotiations

In many markets, on many publications, and in other media outlets, there is a direct relationship between the advertising you buy and the coverage your store receives. This can be an express part of the advertising deal or it may just be implied.

Where this sort of pay-for-play deal is explicit, it forms part of the negotiation for your advertising. Understanding that going in makes it possible to get the best available deal. In print media, ads are either sold by the column inch or as a fraction of a page. Usually, the larger the ad the less expensive it will be on a unit basis. As well, if you are willing to commit to a number of weeks or months there is usually a discount.

A couple of basic print ad negotiating points: Get the best price the ad salesperson is able to offer and then wait a few days until the newspaper or magazine is at its deadline for advertising. Most print publications will be willing to knock off a few percent just to get your ad in their publication that week or month. Second, ask for a cash discount if you can pay cash or with a check before publication. (This works with many other suppliers as well.)

Look for good placement. The lower right hand corner of a page towards the front of a magazine is optimal. In newspapers, look for right hand page placement as well.

If there is going to be an article on your store as part of the deal, make sure that your ad does not appear on the page where the article runs. Ideally, the ad will appear in the front of the magazine or paper and the article will be in the second half. Basically, you want people to see your store twice.

Where there is no explicit connection between advertising and editorial coverage you can certainly make it clear you look forward to news and service coverage of your store. Mention your opening date and ask, specifically, which of the reporters should be sent press releases. There is a Chinese wall between advertising and editorial but there are also a lot of pretty big holes in most of those walls. Make it clear to your ad rep that you expect coverage.

Tip: With print magazines, get to know the ad manager and tell him or her that if they have extra space in a particular edition you are interested if they sell it to you at a steep discount. Make sure you have your ad at the publication in the size you have bought and a couple of other useful sizes. When the print deadline approaches the ad manager may have a quarter or an eighth of a page which is empty and would go to a non-revenue "house" ad. Your ad can fill that space at 50 percent of the regular rate.

Radio and television advertising generally doesn't make a lot of sense for a single location store. Leave aside the fact such advertising is often not permitted under the regulations; broadcast media are not particularly focused but are usually very expensive. By all means check the rates but it is unlikely the possible ROI will justify the expense.

Local blogs and other websites offer an interesting and sometimes very effective way of reaching your target audience. Plus, in most cases, advertising on a blog is relatively inexpensive. Each blog will price its ads its own way, but it is a good idea to pay a flat rate rather than one based on impressions. A local blog with 500 visitors a day focused on the area or city where you are located may be a bargain compared to print or broadcast advertising. However, make sure it is a blog which might appeal to your target audience: A blog aimed at fundamentalist Christians may have huge numbers but they are not likely to be the people who will want to buy your pot.

With blogs and local media, make it clear that you would love to be interviewed on legal marijuana and that if they need news comments you would be happy to oblige. Your mission is to get your store's name in the paper, and being available for comment on marijuana issues will make that happen.

Security

7

It would be nice to think that a retail marijuana shop is no more under threat than any other retail operation. The reality is otherwise. Along with the normal issues of shoplifting and employee theft, the marijuana business has its own, specific security issues.

In the United States, the threat is multiplied by the reluctance of banks to deal with marijuana clients. While this is, slowly, changing, the fact is that in many cases a retail marijuana shop will do all of its business in cash. No credit cards, no debit cards: We've discussed the difficulties this poses for day-to-day operations like paying bills, employees, and taxes but the cash itself is a significant issue. A small, but successful pot shop can see $10,000 a day across its counters. A larger concern can see 500 sales a day at an average of $40 a transaction, for a cash handle of $20,000 plus. That much cash on hand makes a marijuana shop a target.

The product itself is also seen as valuable. The fact is that compared to jewelry or high-end electronics, marijuana is not all that valuable, but people don't become thieves because they are particularly bright. In the thief's world, marijuana is seen as valuable and so a store with lots of pot, or the grow operation which supports that store, appears to be an attractive target.

How attractive? When recreational marijuana was first legalized in Colorado roughly 50 percent of the licensed stores and grow-ops were either subject to

armed robbery or break-ins. As you might guess, demand for security services shot up.

The other element of security is regulatory. In some jurisdictions, the regulations have as their goal the tracking of every bit of marijuana, "from seed to sale." The underlying rationales for this level of intrusion are usually to prevent leakage in the system and to make sure minors are shut out. A distant third rationale is to ensure quality control.

Governments, faced with the mandate to legalize and regulate marijuana, have tended to take a closed-system approach. In simplest terms, the regulatory rules seek to set up systems where every element of production and sale can be monitored. This is intended to keep track of the pot in the system, but also to allow the government to know exactly who has access to the pot every step of the way. The intention is to ensure that only vetted, non-criminals are involved in the pot growing and distribution within a jurisdiction.

The single most important thing about security is that it needs to be considered from the earliest stages of your planning. Budgeting for a security consultant early on will tend to save you money down the road. Understanding security costs and building them into your capital budget and your projections will save you from unpleasant shocks.

Most important, unless you have real expertise in the form of actually being or having been a security professional or trained law enforcement professional, security is not something you can do yourself. The security arrangements for your marijuana business will have a direct impact on the physical safety of your employees, customers, and yourself. Getting the right advice early in the project can, literally, save your life.

1. Regulatory Requirements

Each jurisdiction will have its own regulations surrounding security. Your lawyer will be able to direct you to the relevant rules and regulations, however your lawyer will not be able to tell you how to comply with the regulations. This is where a security consultant is important.

Security regulations look complex when you read them but are, for the most part, quite straightforward in practice. They deal with people, licensed product, and places. This is usually accomplished by making a distinction between "limited access areas" and the rest of the premises. Where there is a requirement for video monitoring, that requirement is almost always designed to allow the regulator to check to make sure the people/product/place rules are being followed.

Regulatory security requirements are compatible with but are not a substitute for actual security. Simply because your marijuana retail location is fully compliant with your jurisdiction's regulations does not mean that you are secure from external threats.

The design of security regulations is about controlling and monitoring individuals' access to the licensed product and ensuring that that product leaves a verifiable paper (well, database) trail as it moves from seed to sale.

The regulations can be very detailed and very demanding. In Colorado, for example, every plant has to be RDIF tagged and traced through cultivation to sale in an approved Marijuana Inventory Tracking System (MITS). There is a requirement for every marijuana outlet to have at least one trained MITS administrator. The MITS information, on every plant in the grow-op and the store is directly available to the regulator.

To ensure that the people involved can be identified, every person in the designated limited access areas — basically, anyone behind the counter — has to wear a current license badge issued by the regulator, in a plainly visible manner above the waist.

Under the Colorado regulations "Camera coverage is required for all Limited Access Areas, point-of-sale areas, security rooms, all points of ingress and egress to Limited Access Areas, all areas where Retail Marijuana or Retail Marijuana Product is displayed for sale, and all points of ingress and egress to the exterior of the Licensed Premises." The point of sale coverage must be sufficient to allow the "recording of the customer(s) and employee(s) facial features with sufficient clarity to determine identity."

The video recording equipment has to be located in an authorized entry only, secure surveillance room and records of all servicing must be kept.

Colorado regulations require that marijuana retail stores have professionally installed and monitored security systems and commercial grade locks.

The Colorado system, being one of the first out of the gate, has been influential in other jurisdictions which legalize recreational marijuana. If the regulatory objective is to create a closed system with positive vetting of every person in contact with the marijuana products until a confirmed sale occurs, this is a seemingly effective system. It certainly answers the in-store bureaucratic imperative.

2. Security and Loss Prevention of Cash and Product

Security required by regulations is a sometimes useful first step in securing your business. Running this kind of business in states like Colorado where there is an employee licensing scheme — with extensive background checks

— can be reassuring when it comes to hiring decisions. The inventory tracking requirements and the video surveillance should reduce pilferage; good locks and alarm systems will deter opportunistic burglars. Well-constructed safe rooms and serious safes will, to a degree, protect your cash. But for all of those precautions and compliance with the regulations, there will be gaps.

A security professional will be able to identify some of the gaps in your systems and correct them. However, as long as there are physical products and large quantities of cash there will be points of vulnerability.

The largest point of vulnerability would be if you fail to include security as part of the DNA of your marijuana retail operation. Having the best alarm system in the world is useless unless you remember to turn it on every night. The same is true of every other security procedure; use it or it's useless.

While the security demanded by the regulators regarding in-store product and people is extensive and will tend to encourage excellent security practices, the regulators do not tend to deal with two major issues: transporting products from off-site locations and dealing with cash in large quantities.

Here is where private security companies offer services which, while sometimes expensive, offer a good deal of protection and peace of mind.

Security companies offer a variety of services, though it may be difficult to find a security company in a smaller town. Having an in-store security guard may sound like overkill, but larger establishments may find this a wise investment. Simply seeing a security guard can deter casual thieves and the security guard can be present when product arrives and cash departs. However, putting an untrained 21 year old in a uniform with the word "security" on it is often worse than useless.

Some jurisdictions require on-premises security guards and have strict requirements including that guards be older than 25 years of age, have military or police training, undertake regular training, and are armed. This means that a marijuana retail outlet will have to contract with a third party for its security personnel, which is expensive and needs to be budgeted.

In a perfect world you would have several cash pick-ups a day by armored truck, so that your cash is not on the premises. In the absence of banking arrangements you have to have a safe place for this cash; off premises is nearly always safer than on, but pickups are very expensive.

A more realistic solution is a cash management system which clears the tills regularly, counts the money, and ensures that it is secured in a serious safe. This has to be built into your cost estimate and your standard business operations. Here, again, the advice of a security consultant can be invaluable.

The hazards of a cash-based business don't end with securing the cash. Businesses have bills — rent, taxes, wages — and paying each in cash creates another set of vulnerabilities and costs which other businesses don't have.

Product shipments mean that thousands of dollars of inventory moves from one location to another. It is important to keep this in perspective: Truckloads of goods worth far more than that are delivered to retailers all over the US and Canada without incident. However, again from the thieves' perspective, there is something very attractive about a shipment of drugs.

Something as simple as having a secure delivery area may not add a great deal to the cost of your retail store but will help keep shipments safe. Having a secure room where shipments are checked and product entered into inventory makes a lot of sense and may, in fact, be required by regulations.

In many jurisdictions, legalization has brought specialized security firms which deal with both cash and product. They have made it their business to understand the specific security risks faced by marijuana retail stores and growing operations and have systems to minimize that risk. However, these firms tend to focus on businesses located in major cities. If you are in the suburbs or in smaller cities and towns your options may be limited.

Simple strategies such as limiting the inventory which is on the sales floor can reduce potential losses. So can a rule which limits customers to examining one product at a time. These strategies will limit grab-and-go thefts, but a well-planned armed robbery will trump this level of precaution.

External threats are one side of the security operation. The other is recognizing that even vetted, criminal-record-checked employees can be tempted by the sheer amount of cash or the easy accessibility of marijuana products. In principle, rigid, Colorado-style inventory control and video surveillance should keep employee theft of product minimal. But as any bar owner will tell you, simple things like overpouring for friends can kill your margins. Employee theft needs to be monitored and acted upon immediately, particularly the sort of overpouring which does not really seem like theft at all.

The issue here is more cultural than criminal: It is very much human nature to want to do your friends proud or make sure that your regular customers are happy with their purchases, and many of us think that adding a little extra can't hurt. If that attitude becomes part of your store's culture, your margins will shrink, your control over the critical Cost of Sales number will crumble and, where the regulator is monitoring from seed to sale, you will have regulatory problems in a matter of months if not weeks.

A good security consultant will give you the tools to enforce a strict weight-to-sale regime. In some cases that will mean smaller quantities are prepackaged so that your frontline employees never touch the product. With edibles, oils, and tinctures, this is really the only way the product can be sold.

At the same time, a retail marijuana store owner may want to consider ways that employees, in a completely traceable way, can offer small discounts to good customers and friends. Being able to upsell an eighth of an ounce to a quarter with a few percent off the final price may make a lot of business sense as far as making customers feel they're getting a good deal and giving employees a sense of empowerment.

The cash side of things is much more straightforward. In the US, because of the banks' recalcitrance, much of the marijuana business has to be conducted in cash, which means employees see thousands of dollars come across the counter. The temptation to figure out clever ways for $20 here and there to not make it to the till or the counting machine is significant.

Retailers have been dealing with sticky fingered employees for centuries and the fact is that loss reduction is the result of a set of procedures and practices enforced absolutely and without exception.

Loss prevention begins at the hiring stage. While states like Colorado require licenses for every person involved in the marijuana trade, and getting one of those licenses involves a full criminal record check, this should be a beginning of a vetting process not the end. Doing the reference checks, making the phone calls, actually talking to a potential employee's last supervisor is time consuming. Doing a credit check might seem intrusive but it may be very revealing. Yes, do look online and on social media.

One of the best predictors of loss experience is staff turnover: As a brand new enterprise, your marijuana store needs to pay attention to staff retention, which means making hiring decisions which include issues like stability, ties to the community, family, and commitment. (At the same time you must be careful to avoid interview questions which are contrary to law.)

Loss prevention needs to be part of the training program and staff manual each employee undergoes before your store is open. Your procedures for inventory handling and cash control need to be walked through until they are literally the defaults your employees go to. Managers have to be on top of the key points in every transaction; not to spot theft, rather to ensure that the required practices are adhered to. It is much better for your store and for your employees to have minor errors in required procedure detected and corrected before they become occasions for loss.

For most employees, knowing that there is video surveillance of every transaction is something of a deterrent to theft, but that deterrent effect diminishes as time passes. Managers' "eyes on" is not as ignorable as video; it is a daily reminder to do the right thing the right way.

Recognizing that your retail marijuana store is a deeply regulated business needs to be part of every employee's training. By emphasizing that the rules cover inventory and therefore everything to do with the sale of that inventory, you bring cash handling into the regulatory frame. Essentially, you make it clear to your employees and managers that you risk your license if there is any discrepancy in inventory.

The one thing which a marijuana retail store owner has in his or her favor is that the people who work in pot shops and dispensaries almost always want to work there. Especially in the early days of legalization in a particular jurisdiction, there are usually many people who have been part of the underground cannabis culture who see working in the regulated, legal marijuana world as more than a job. While this is not going to eliminate the possibility of dishonesty, it will tend to promote good will and a positive culture in a marijuana retail store. Working with that sense of mission gives an owner a measure of security which can't be bought.

3. Security Is a Cost of Doing Business

Security costs cut into margins by driving up the cost of sales. Where those security costs — things like inventory control, video surveillance, secure storage, alarm systems, proper locks — are mandated by the regulations in your jurisdiction, they are simply a cost of doing business. The cost of a security consultant early in the process is pretty much unavoidable and needs to be budgeted for, as is a secure safe.

Where business decisions are called for is in the level of ongoing security. Having a single, trained, professional security guard on premises during business hours can run as high as $120,000 a year. From a business risk perspective that expense may not be justified or, for that matter, sustainable. Security firms in Colorado charge between $5,000 and $15,000 per month for basic protection for a retail marijuana outlet.

Investing in passive security — hardened windows, secure doors and locks, an excellent safe, secure safe rooms, and secure product storage — is an upfront cost but one likely to pay for itself because these measures act as a deterrent. Add staff policies which emphasize security and a culture of integrity and you may be able to improve security. Choosing an easier to secure location in a low crime area can reduce risks further.

Working with a security professional to improve your security operations and to make recommendations for on-site security is likely a needed investment. As long as it is difficult or impossible to bank the cash from your operations and to accept credit and debit cards, the marijuana business will face increased risk from robbery. Understanding that risk and building a provision for such losses into your financial and business plans may make the difference between the success and failure of your marijuana retail business.

4. Insurance as Security

While you may not be able to bank your proceeds, you can insure your marijuana business, and, in fact, you should. Any business open to the public needs standard business insurance which covers the various liabilities which you incur when you invite the public into your premises. Display racks can fall over and floors can be slippery. Property insurance will be required by your landlord and it makes sense to insure your fixtures and equipment against theft, fire, and even vandalism.

General liability insurance, which protects you from legal liability arising from your products, the actions of your employees, and injuries suffered by members of the public while in your store, makes sense as well. (Although, the question of product liability with respect to the sale of marijuana is by no means settled.)

While some insurers have been reluctant to enter the medical and recreational marijuana markets, others have seen the industry as a new and rapidly expanding market. Finding specialist insurers for marijuana in your jurisdiction takes 30 seconds on Google. Most have rules as to the security of your premises and requirements for locks and video surveillance which are in line with the regulatory requirements of your jurisdiction.

Good insurance is not a substitute for physical security and a culture which takes security and integrity seriously, but it is an excellent backstop and will prevent a robbery or burglary from putting you out of business.

5. Canada

The security and insurance situation for marijuana retail outlets in Canada is complicated by the fact that, as this book is written, cannabis is still illegal for recreational use and the medical marijuana regulations have been struck down in federal court.

The situation is further complicated by the federal government's promise to legalize marijuana. This promise has been slow to take effect with a task force to look into the issue and report back in 2017. This has not stopped hundreds of medical marijuana dispensaries from springing up across the country. The law is in a state of flux and these entrepreneurs are taking advantage of the fact that many police forces and Crown attorneys see very little upside to prosecuting cases which will fare badly before a judge.

The legal and regulatory ambiguity of marijuana in Canada has not stopped thieves from hitting pop-up, ad hoc dispensaries. Daylight robberies where thieves use guns or knives to force salespeople to turn over cash and product are depressingly regular occurrences.

On the upside, while the major banks in Canada are reluctant to extend banking facilities to marijuana businesses, this reluctance has not extended to the nation's many credit unions. This means that the problem of an all-cash business is much reduced in many Canadian jurisdictions. Credit unions are also able to provide the machines required for the dispensaries to take credit and debit cards. Simply by removing the cash pile problem, the credit unions have made marijuana dispensaries significantly safer.

Despite the robberies it is unlikely that a competent security consultant would recommend armed security in a Canadian retail marijuana store. Canadian law allows for armed security in very limited circumstances and store protection is usually outside those circumstances. Unarmed security may be an option but a more likely counter-robbery strategy would be the installation of panic buttons which summon the police.

While cash may be dealt with in a more or less normal way, the product itself needs a degree of protection. Secure storage facilities, such as, possibly, a large safe in a secure room are prudent. Video surveillance may make sense particularly at the counters and checkouts.

Where the marijuana retail store is operating as a medical dispensary — a category which does not enjoy any legal existence at the federal level — making sure that customers have a "Medical Document for the Access to Cannabis for Medical Purposes Regulations" certificate prior to purchasing their marijuana is seen as important. In the process the store might also want to see picture ID which will confirm the age of the customer. Done properly this ID/Certificate check on entry to the store can improve security.

Finally, the largely unregulated Canadian market means that retail store owners do not have obvious, legal sources of wholesale supply. The one place they cannot buy wholesale is from regulated medical marijuana growers who are restricted by law to selling directly to medical marijuana users by mail order. Other sources of supply will likely include licensed grow-ops which have continued to operate under the previous medical marijuana regime. And, of course, there are criminal grow-ops which are happy to sell to pop-up dispensaries.

From a security perspective, a Canadian marijuana dispensary owner is likely at greater risk dealing with the criminals who provide the supply than from potential thieves. Marijuana sales from illegal grow-ops are a cash transaction with the owner bringing the cash and picking up the product. It is not difficult to see how such a transaction can go wrong. Looking for reliable, non-criminal sources of supply is a key piece of a security strategy for a Canadian retail marijuana store.

Human Resources

A great store will try to have great people working for it. Finding, screening, hiring, and managing those great people is a huge part of an owner's value-add to his or her business, but it is also a bit of a legal minefield.

As a marijuana retail store owner you need to plan your hiring moves well before you open your store. You need to research your jurisdiction's employment laws and consult with your lawyer to make sure you understand how to hire the right people the right way.

1. Contract Employees or At Will

Depending on the employment law of your jurisdiction, an employee can be offered a contract or be taken on "at will." Walking through the advantages and disadvantages of both situations with an employment lawyer will let you know what your options are and, most important, how you deal with your worker may change the legal nature of the relationship.

A worker hired at will has some basic rights under your jurisdiction's employment law. They are often very basic indeed: the right to be paid for work performed, the right to holidays, and a maximum number of hours worked per week for base pay. What an at-will worker does not have is security of tenure. He or she can often be dismissed without cause and with very short notice for any reason or no reason at all (but not for an unlawful reason; really, talk to a lawyer).

A worker under an employment contract has the rights set out in that contract. These rights can be quite significant and are usually the subject of negotiation. Issues like overtime, payment for working statutory holidays, grounds for termination, benefits, and so on are all potentially up for negotiation; so are things like job descriptions and duties.

Generally, the more responsible positions in your store should have contracts of employment.

2. Hiring Staff

Even a very small marijuana store will need more than the owner to perform all of the functions a retail store requires. This is especially true where there are significant regulatory rules about the sale, storage, and tracking of the marijuana products.

Some jurisdictions require employees in marijuana businesses to be licensed. From the owner's perspective this requirement will mean that you must either only hire people who have their license or who are eligible to get that license. Which, in turn, means making the license requirement clear in any advertising you do for the jobs in your store.

No matter what the marijuana licensing requirements of your jurisdiction, you will be hiring people who will be handling relatively valuable product and cash. You can train a person to use your systems and teach a person about your products; character and work habits are not as easily taught.

As we discussed in the Chapter 8 on security, part of a successful hiring process is a close vetting of applicants. Before you even interview a person you need to check references, gain permission to do a credit check, where possible do a criminal record check, look at potential hires' social media, and don't be shy about Googling them as well. This is time consuming and costs money, but it will let you avoid hires who might be bad for your business.

It makes sense to narrow the field by using a standard application form, even for management positions. While you have to conform to federal and state or provincial employment laws, a good application form which asks for more background information than businesses usually ask for can save you time. Questions about previous employment are very useful. So are questions about residence; not just current address but also addresses for a number of years previous.

Asking about volunteer work, community involvement, and nonbusiness skills can be very revealing. An employee with deep connections to his or her community demonstrates a stability and engagement which are valuable. So are the connections a potential employee brings to the business.

Interviewing potential employees gives an owner a sense of who they are but also what sort of energy and attitude they are likely to bring. Interviews are tough for everyone and it is often a good idea to build in a break. It is a simple technique where you get the more formal elements out of the way in the first 10–20 minutes and then take a few minutes away from the interview before moving on to the more subjective elements; the conversation, as it were. A break works because it drains a lot of the tension from the situation. When you resume it is no longer a "cold" situation; rather both of you are over the awkwardness many people feel on first meeting someone.

There is no right person for a job in a marijuana retail store, especially your store. Hiring staff is difficult and people you think will be a great fit turn out to be awful while people you are initially hesitant about wind up having unexpected talents. The best a business owner can hope for is to avoid hiring the dishonest or the unmotivated.

3. The Hiring Decision and Papering the Deal

Once you have gone through the application, screening, and interview process you will, you hope, have found some great people to work in your marijuana retail store. You have your list and you have figured out which people will fit which position.

Making an informal offer of employment is fine but it is amazing how often misunderstandings can arise from a simple phone call or conversation.

An offer of employment should be in writing and the basic form should be run by your lawyer. You are creating a relationship with rights and responsibilities and these need to be clear from the outset. Even before the offer is made, a file on the potential employee should be started with his or her application materials, notes from the interview, whatever screening you have done, and any licensing information all in its place. In fact, such files should be kept for every applicant, successful or not.

The offer of employment need not be elaborate; but it should include the position the person is being hired for, the wage or salary being offered, the hours expected and, where applicable, a nondisclosure agreement (more on this in section 4.) Your lawyer will be able to vet your offer and advise you if it constitutes a contract of employment which you may or may not want to have constructed. At a minimum, your future employee should sign the offer acknowledging receipt and return a copy for your records.

An offer of employment should include a reference to your employee manual. You should also take the time to send rejection notices to unsuccessful applicants to eliminate any possibility that they are confused about there being an employment relationship.

4. Nondisclosure Agreements

When you hire someone you are going to need to let him or her in on a good deal of confidential information; everything from the financial performance of your store, your suppliers, your inventory control systems, your security arrangements, client lists, and the intellectual property embodied in your approach to selling marijuana. What if he or she doesn't work out as an employee?

Worst-case scenario is that your now former employee walks down the street to your competitors and gives them the benefit of your confidential information. Because they are no longer your employee there is very little you can do about that unless you have, as part of the offer of employment process, had them sign a nondisclosure agreement (NDA). An NDA — drafted carefully by your lawyer — should be designed to survive the end of the employment relationship. It prohibits your now former employee from disclosing information to which he or she has become privy during the course of employment (or contract if you are dealing with contract workers.)

Having an effective NDA in effect from the day your new employee starts work will give you at least some protection from the disclosure of your confidential information to third parties. Your business and trade secrets are almost certainly worth the small additional fee a lawyer will charge to create a document which will protect your business.

Noncompete agreements are also potentially worthwhile, particularly for key employees. However, these must be very carefully drafted in conformity with your jurisdiction's employment laws. Seek legal advice and expect to pay for the lawyer's time spent analyzing your particular situation.

5. Employee Manual and Training

It is tempting to think that because you only plan to have a few employees an employee manual is something you can skip for now. Nothing could be further from the truth. In fact, in several jurisdictions, marijuana retail businesses are required, as a condition of their licenses, to have an employee manual.

A basic employee manual — perhaps five or six pages — outlines the expectations you have of your employees including your policies regarding —

- holidays,
- training,
- insurance,
- payroll procedures,

- absences,
- dress code,
- compliance with applicable regulations,
- anti-harassment and anti-discrimination mechanisms,
- employee evaluations, and
- employee and customer complaints.

Arriving on time, taking direction from yourself and your managers, following standard procedures, and ensuring employees conduct themselves in compliance with all applicable regulations is a good start. Being clear from the outset that the employee is to follow the policies in the employee manual can avoid some of the more difficult situations which arise in the employment relationship.

An employer/employee relationship is a legal relationship and — implicitly or explicitly — gives rise to legal rights and responsibilities for both parties. From the day you make a formal offer of employment — and it should be formal and in writing — you as an employer assume the obligations of an employer. You need to know what those obligations are in your jurisdiction so spend the time to research it ahead of time.

Open for Business

9

Every store opening is a scramble. All your work, all your investment, your hiring, license applications, supplies, and your fixtures are on the line when you open your store's doors for the first time. Will you be ready?

Probably not as ready as you'd like to be. What this chapter is designed to do is aim you in the right direction. You may not be able to eliminate every minor error, but you can and should eliminate any errors which would have a significant impact on your business.

1. Checklist and Timeline

You have cleared all the regulatory hurdles; secured a legal source of marijuana (either you will buy it wholesale or you will grow it yourself); found the perfect location; have legally compliant signage; secure storage; and a security protocol. You are ready to sell marijuana.

Well, almost. The fact is that in virtually every jurisdiction where marijuana has been fully legalized and regulated there are procedures you have to follow before you can legally open your doors, even after you have obtained your license.

For example, in Colorado you have to have an approved seed-to-sale inventory monitoring system in place. You and all your employees must have received occupational licenses (a.k.a., pot badges) from the Marijuana Enforcement Division. Your store must be licensed. You have to display the store license and make sure that your employees all wear their pot badges at all times. You have to have a video monitoring system which is compliant with the regulations, and you need a designated person to ensure that system is operating and recording properly.

Plus, depending on your jurisdiction, there are various pre-opening inspections both from the marijuana perspective and at the municipal level. Getting to the point of opening requires keeping track of a lot of moving pieces. At least a month before you plan to open, it is a good idea to make an opening checklist with the items to be done along with the names and numbers of the contacts for each of those items.

Along with the regulatory items, this checklist should include all of the must-have items for the store opening: staff, cash registers, store fixtures, products for sale, security, marketing, advertising, a cash float, change. It should be a complete list of all things essential to your opening. As the owner, this list is your responsibility, but it is an excellent idea to share it with your managers and your staff well before opening day. Ask them to review it and make suggestions.

Attached to that checklist there should be a timeline counting backward and forward from your projected opening day.

Building a good timeline needs to start months before your projected opening date. The fact is there are lead times for everything from your advertising to your packaging to larger items like staff training and systems checks. Some of the items on your timeline are one-offs: You only design your packaging once. Others, like marketing, start before you open and are constants in your business.

By drafting your checklist and timeline at the earliest possible moment you give yourself the time and the organization required to actually open your store with a minimum amount of last-minute panic. The fewer things left to the last minute the fewer things will go wrong. Be prepared: The best checklist and the most complete timeline will miss something. You and your managers will have to be ready to improvise on the day.

2. Soft or Hard Launch

As the owner of a retail marijuana store it is mainly up to you whether you want to make a splash on your opening day or you simply want to slide into the marketplace with limited fanfare. However, you may be restricted by the regulations in your jurisdiction from offering opening day (or any kind of) specials on the marijuana or associated merchandise.

Whether you intend to go big on opening day or keep it pretty casual, the reality is that you almost always need to soft launch a few days before your official opening. A soft launch is just that: It is an opportunity to open your store to the public but without the pressure of an Opening Day launch and all the fanfare that creates.

You can always have an official opening day a week or even a month after you have soft-launched, and even before you open your doors to the public, it is a very good idea to have a couple of training days for your staff.

Training days and soft launches let you test each of your systems in low stress situations. On a training day you might want to walk through various transactions with staff taking turns to role play the customers. By doing simulated transactions you can test your point of sale equipment. You can practice your cash management procedures. You can work through the restocking process without a lineup of eager customers clamoring for their marijuana. While you are doing your simulated transactions it may be worthwhile to have your security consultant on premises watching live and on video.

When you are sure you and your staff are ready, where legal, (check the regulations), you may want to have a private opening where people are invited for snacks and a glass of wine and you are set up to sell your products if they wish to purchase them. If that goes well then you may decide to open for a few hours to the general public. This is the real test: Making sure that your systems work with people off the street.

All this takes time and, because you are going to have staff in the store for training and the eventual soft launch, money. However, it is time and money well spent if you are able to ensure that all of your systems, from inventory control to cash management to customer service, work well and have the bugs ironed out.

3. Community

Every retail business is part of a community. Even if your location is relatively isolated, the fact that you are selling cannabis products will mean that you are seen as part of the marijuana community which has various consequences. If, however, you are in a shopping district, your community extends well beyond cannabis culture.

When you open your store for business you are adding your business to the ecosystem of businesses, services, government, and the public they serve. Being aware of your place in that ecosystem can be a huge part of a successful business.

There may be some discomfort with the entire idea of a retail marijuana store in some communities. Not everyone considers legal marijuana a good thing and it is important to acknowledge this. As well, in some shopping districts there will be a concern that your marijuana dispensary or store will attract undesirable customers to the area. Understanding and responding to those concerns is good business and good community relations.

Where you are putting a store into a preexisting shopping area it only makes sense to get to know the owners and workers of the stores surrounding yours. Simply walking around your neighborhood with a business card and a great attitude well before you open will let people express any concerns they may have. Listening carefully is a great first step, but you might also want to invite other retailers to your store before you open. Once they understand that your marijuana store is a retail store just like theirs with the same issues of merchandising, security, and marketing, you and your store will look much less alien.

It is also a good idea to invite the police, community workers, and other community leaders to your store before you open. If they are confident that you are running a legitimate, legal, compliant business they are more likely to accept a legal marijuana store in their community.

Community relations efforts don't stop the day you open your doors. Becoming part of your community — doing things like contributing to community charities, advertising in local publications, shopping locally even if it costs a bit extra, joining the Chamber of Commerce and business district committees — all build ties. Wherever possible, hiring locally can be an excellent way to cement ties.

Pay attention to the political issues in your community and municipality. It is surprising how many retail businesspeople ignore municipal politics only to find themselves hurt by tax and zoning changes they could have prevented. If you have an area representative on your city council, make a point of meeting him or her. You don't have to be political but you have to pay attention to politics, particularly at the local level.

Ultimately a marijuana retail store and its owner need to be embedded in the community. Instead of being seen as a dangerous, drug dealing outsider, a marijuana shop should fit seamlessly into its surroundings.

3.1 A good neighbor

In Chapter 6 where we discussed branding, we looked at how design choices can really make a lot of difference as to how well your store blends into the neighborhood. Spending a bit of extra money to create a welcoming, visually pleasing storefront will give your marijuana store a bit of curb appeal.

Equally worthwhile is a rather old-fashioned shopkeeper's attitude toward keeping not only the interior of your store clean, but making sure that the windows are always spotless and the sidewalk is swept a couple of times a day. Bringing pride of ownership to the street on which you are located makes you a good neighbor.

If you are in a row of stores, make the effort to get to know your immediate neighbors. You'll need their forbearance as you bang your shop into shape, plus they will have local knowledge which is incredibly valuable. Put a few decent lunches into your pre-opening budget and make sure you invite all your neighbors to whatever you decide will be your opening.

Try to be helpful but don't try too hard. Your neighbors have been in business for some time. They probably have most of their needs sorted out. Being friendly and cooperative is usually enough when you are starting out.

At the same time, your neighbors will likely have a variety of people they like working with for things like maintenance, snow removal, locksmithing, security services and alarm systems, and even store fixtures and lighting. Asking around is never a bad idea and often a neighboring store will appreciate the opportunity to throw business in friends' directions.

It is also not a bad idea to, where permitted, offer a neighborhood discount for your products. It does not have to be much. As little as 5 or 10 percent off is enough to invite the neighborhood to patronize your store. Of course, by the same token, make sure that you target your own buying to your neighbors' stores. Small gestures will enhance your reputation.

4. So Now Your Store Is Open

Your checklist is complete, and your media presence and web presence is established. You opened the doors, and people are coming to your store and buying your product.

There is an awful temptation to see the "open for business" moment as the end of the journey. In fact, it is the real beginning. You are in the marijuana business, but for how long?

Sorry to be a buzz kill, but the vast majority of small businesses fail. They fail for a variety of reasons but all of those reasons come down to a failure to actually make money.

The math is brutal. You take your investment in the store, your stock in trade, your weekly and monthly expenses, and you look at your gross sales revenue. Are you selling more than it costs you to keep the doors open? If not, what is your burn rate and how much money do you have to subsidize your monthly loss? Have you paid your taxes? Have you paid your staff? Do you have enough money to restock the shop for next month? Welcome to retail.

Growing Your Business

10

Once you have your retail marijuana store's doors open the real work of retail begins. Bringing the customers in the door, making sure you have products they want to buy, hiring new staff, training, marketing: Retail is thousands of little details.

Plus, to keep your investment secure, you need to ensure that you remain in compliance with the regulations in your jurisdiction. Those regulations may change over time and you need to be aware of changes and plan for them.

Finally you need to look forward to increasing the profitability of your operation, possibly expanding and, because it is never too soon, thinking about and planning your possible exit from the business.

But first, a look at operations.

1. Getting to Breakeven

With your first sale to the public, you are in business. But you are in business behind a big pile of what can most easily be understood as debt, which has been used to pay for your store, your goods for sale, your security, your website, your advertising, and so on. Your first sale is the first entry on the credit side of the ledger.

Your accountant will explain it all to you but in thinking about starting your marijuana business you need to be clear about how the money works in that business. There are a lot of ways of doing financial analysis but the most intuitive is to look at gross sales and then start making deductions. This is not the correct way to look at money in your business but it will give you a feel for the numbers.

If you sell a $1,000 worth of goods on a particular day the first deduction you need to make is the Cost of Goods Sold (COGS). If you are buying your marijuana from a wholesaler you will have a very clear idea of the COGS for that particular product in its many varieties. If part of your sales are edibles and another part delivery devices you will have a clear idea of what the COGS is for those lines of product as well.

To make this example simple let's assume that your $1,000 in gross sales involved goods which cost you $500, which leaves you with $500 in gross revenue. Now, from that gross revenue number you deduct the costs of your store's operation on the day the revenue was earned. Rent, insurance, wages, security, utilities, breakage, marketing, advertising, property taxes: Every single expense your store has on the day it earns the revenue is deducted from the gross revenue to leave you with your net revenue.

That net revenue is what you have to pay down the debt you incurred setting up your store. And that is completely ignoring taxes which, in fact, can all but or even eliminate your net revenue depending on your jurisdiction.

As a retail marijuana store owner you have to work hard at increasing your net revenue because it is the only actual money your store will generate.

Breakeven is the point where your sales are sufficient to cover all of your ongoing expenses. But breakeven does not put you in a net revenue position. It just means you are not running up more debt.

In a simple business model there is only one source of revenue: sales. In principle, growing your sales will get your business to breakeven and beyond. However, that assumes that you have your pricing right and that you make more on a sale than that sale costs you.

Net margin — that is, the difference between your cost of goods plus cost of sales and the price of your goods — is a powerful tool for looking at what your store is doing. Net margin is determined by three things: the price you can sell your goods at, the cost of those goods, and the cost of running your business.

As a store owner you can set your prices at whatever level you want, however, unless you enjoy an effective local monopoly, your competitor down the street can set her prices marginally lower and draw your customers to her store. This means, in reality, marijuana itself becomes a commodity once it is legalized and the margins available to any given store will tend to shrink due to price competition.

The good news is that the wholesale price of marijuana post legalization also tends to decline as more people enter the growing business and get better at it. (In fact, Washington State has experienced a glut of marijuana at the wholesale level since legalization.)

Wholesale prices will be driven by the usual tug of war between demand and supply, but a knowledgeable store owner will develop relationships with wholesalers in order to get good prices and also to get deals on specific products. The fact is that growing marijuana is not a perfect science. A grower/wholesaler may find himself with more of a particular strain than he can easily sell. With a good relationship a store owner can take advantage of these situations and get wholesale product at less than the usual price, which means that if the store keeps its price steady its margins will go up in these situations.

Where regulations allow, a store owner may find that she achieves higher margins on other marijuana products such as distillates, oils, and edibles. Or, it may turn out that marijuana and its derivative products have less margin than the glassware, vaporizers, and other paraphernalia which some jurisdictions allow recreational pot shops to stock.

The Cost of Goods Sold (COGS) is one piece of the puzzle; another piece is the store's overall running expenses. Items such as rent and insurance are pretty much locked in, however wages, advertising, some elements of security, and even utilities can be controlled and adjusted to fit circumstances and experience. Reducing these expenses will often have a significant impact on your net margins.

A lot of the issues around running expenses are only resolvable in light of experience. What are the right staffing levels for your store? Chances are you will need more sales staff at some points in the week and less at others. Tracking your daily and hourly sales over a few weeks or months will let you deploy staff most effectively. You may discover, for example, that you have next to no sales on Monday mornings. In that case, you can reduce costs by opening at noon on Monday.

Streamlining customer service, prepackaging certain marijuana products, and providing printed information on strains and featured items can all help reduce expenses.

Finally, making sure that your sales staff know which of your products are higher margin can significantly boost your net revenue. Upselling to customers or suggesting a high-margin accessory when they are purchasing marijuana can boost revenue and, more importantly, increase your net.

Paying close attention to Cost of Goods sold, operating expenses, and margins can all get your marijuana retail store to breakeven and beyond. This requires a real commitment from the store owner and her managers.

2. Past Breakeven

If all has gone well you will have kept your expenses under control, tried to reduce your COGS, and increased your overall margins. You will find at the end of the month that you have taken in more than you have spent and that your bills are all paid. Congratulations, you are not just in business, you are on your way to a successful business.

Once a retail store is past breakeven it is often time to sit down with your business plan and update it. Now that you know the actual numbers for your capital costs and operating expenses, and you have hard numbers for your sales, you can take a hard look at where you want your business to go and set a course to get there.

Once your marijuana retail store is producing net revenue you have options. One option which should always be considered is to do nothing; basically, continue to operate your business as it is. If you are making the sort of money you wanted to and had projected in your business plan, this option may suit you. This is especially true if you have opportunities in other areas and have nurtured managers you trust to run the business while you go after those opportunities.

Another option arises when you have not reached your projected revenue targets, or you see the opportunity to increase revenue beyond those targets. In both cases there is a strong argument to be made to attempt to increase your revenue. The question is, how? Business expansion can occur in a number of ways. You can invest in more marketing to bring in more customers to buy more of your existing line of products. Or, you can add new product lines in the hope of increasing sales. Either of these alternatives avoids expanding your premises, having to apply for additional licenses for a new location, or having to hire and train new staff.

Reach back to your business plan and take a look at things you had planned to do but which, in the rush to get the store open, you have not done. There are often excellent ideas lurking in business plans. Now you have the experience to be able to assign realistic costs to those ideas and the ability to compare their projected ROI to the ROI your current store is experiencing.

3. Thinking Bigger

There is a natural temptation when you have conceived and opened a successful marijuana retail store to think about opening a second store, or a chain of stores. After all, your initial success has established that you do know what you are doing. Better still, your store's name, brand, and reputation will be likely to make it easier to secure investment if needed, and customers once you open that second location. A lot of the ice breaking with suppliers and consultants will already have been done.

Leveraging your brand and your knowledge may make a lot of sense but it needs to be carefully thought out from a business risk perspective. Everything from the regulatory issues of a new license through to how to raise the capital needs to be examined. A new business plan needs to be written from scratch, because running two or more stores is a very different set of business challenges than running a single store operation. There may be very good reasons why a multi-location option makes sense, but the same level of hardheaded analysis needs to be run on that option.

4. Thinking Smarter

Rather than cloning your store, it is likely that, once you have reached breakeven, looking at your single store operations to find room for expansion and revenue enhancement will yield significant returns. When you are fighting your way to breakeven you have to squeeze every dollar and you will be rightly reluctant to spend on slightly riskier projects. Once you are in a net revenue situation you can afford to be innovative and take a few risks to gain new customers and new revenue.

Can you add value for your customers while still increasing your margins? It depends on your customers, but the general answer is yes. A loyalty program which offers good customers a small discount can be a great start. Once you have a loyalty program operating, think of ways to use it to increase sales of high margin products. Something as simple as a vaporizer sale at the end of a month for loyalty club members only can work. Or, (where legal) if you are able to get a great deal at wholesale on a particular strain, offer a solid discount to your loyalty club members.

Creating a loyalty program is remarkably inexpensive and allows you to do push selling to your best customers. As always, you have to run this past your lawyer for regulatory scrutiny, but if a program can be designed which is legal in your jurisdiction it is a low risk, high return way to expand your business by increasing revenues.

Working with other businesses can create cross-promotional opportunities at a fairly low cost. Bakeries, pizza parlors, or clothing stores geared towards your demographic are all potential partners. In most jurisdictions you are not allowed to provide marijuana for free which means if you want to cross-promote you need to offer a non-marijuana product or a discount where legal. The point is to get your store's name and location out there.

Look at ways to create higher margins on your existing products. Offering a vaporizer starter kit and something to vaporize may seem obvious, but there will always be curious non-pot-smokers who might be interested if it was all made very easy. In addition, create a strain of the month club and make sure that the monthly strain is a negotiated deal with your wholesaler.

Understand that volume and regularity are critical to your success. The Colorado marijuana use study indicated that 20 percent of the users bought 80 percent of the pot. Where you can legally do so, track your own customers and see if these Colorado numbers are true of your store. If they are, how can you attract more heavy users? Refer-a-friend programs are an excellent way to target particular sorts of customers in your store. If you can identify customers who are heavy users it is a good bet they will have friends who may also buy a lot of marijuana. You want those friends to come to your store.

Your job is to continue to innovate. The fact is that where marijuana has been legalized there has been a rush into the retail business. Dozens of small shops open very quickly and compete for customers. Your business survives and thrives because you are constantly looking for ways to reduce costs, increase margins, and bring in new customers.

5. An Exit Strategy

Far too many small businesses have a plan which ends at the point where they are profitable. If they make it that far their owners seem to think that the business will simply continue for years. Too many small-business owners, because they never considered an exit strategy, end up tied to their businesses long after their enthusiasm has died. Worse, because no thought has been given to exiting the business, some critical work needed to sell the business is left undone. So hopefully, you considered your exit strategy as part of your business plan.

Perhaps the most important element in the sale of a business is to recognize and value the actual assets of that business. Many are intangible. What is a recognized brand worth? What is a 500-member loyalty club mailing list worth? What if that list is 5,000 members strong? What is the value of your lead sponsorship of your town's cannabis festival? What about your relationships with your suppliers?

Conventionally, when a business is sold, all of these things are lumped together under "goodwill." However, if you keep track of how you have built up your goodwill and the expenses you have incurred doing it, you will find that things like a loyalty program or a refer-a-friend promotion will become line items to be valued as part of the sale price.

Keeping excellent books is a key piece of getting full value on the sale of your business. You will likely have excellent books simply because of the regulatory requirements to track inventory and sales. You may come to hate your bookkeeper for being a nag about expenses, but you will be grateful when it comes time to value your business.

A good filing system for important documents like licenses and tax receipts near to hand will make the transaction go more smoothly. So will having complete staff files with all of the information a prospective new owner will need in one location. An updated copy of the employee manual is useful. Supply contracts, invoices, a copy of the lease for the premises; there are hundreds of bits of paper every business has that serious purchasers want to see.

As well as keeping your accounts and files up to date, it is a good idea to prepare updated versions of your business plan as your business moves forward. This is an excellent way to measure your progress and make the course corrections new business challenges turn up. It is also a very useful measure of the actual success of your business.

A business plan update need not be complicated. Simply having actual numbers to place beside projections is a good first step. Including new initiatives, new product lines, and marketing strategies, with their attendant projections gives a sense of the history; the story of your business.

Both your accountant and lawyer will be involved in the sale of your business. It's important to give them a heads up as early as possible if you are planning to sell. It is going to take some of their professional time, plus, both may well know people who might be interested in buying.

Finding a buyer may be difficult. Though marijuana may be legal, it is not necessarily a business with which every investor wants to be involved. Plus, a new owner will need to pass the licensing requirements in your jurisdiction. Two potential groups of buyers should be looked at immediately. First, your investors: In many cases investors will make their investment conditional upon a right of first refusal in the event you decide to sell. If they have that right, you cannot deal with other buyers until your investors have waived their rights. The second group are your employees. It would be unusual for an employee, even a senior manager, to have a right to buy the business, but your managers know your business and might well be interested in buying.

In both cases you need to consult your lawyer and consider how best to structure a purchase deal, assuming you have that option. Buying or selling even a simple retail business can be quite complex and good legal and accounting advice can ensure you get what the business is worth and, as important, that you get it in a tax efficient way.

When and if it comes time to sell your marijuana retail store you will have your numbers and you will have your story. In some cases a purchaser will take a very straight-ahead, numbers-driven approach and will not be much interested in your story, but for some purchasers the story is at least as important as the numbers. What worked, what didn't?

In the years you operate your marijuana business you will be constantly learning about your customers, your staff, your suppliers, and your regulators. You will discover which flavors of edibles sell and which gather dust on the shelves. You will discover what gets heavy users in your target demographic through the door.

That knowledge, and those stories, are the value you add to your marijuana store. A smart purchaser will certainly look at the numbers, but she will want to hear your stories and read through your business plan's revisions.

Every business is a story. It has a beginning, middle and, we hope, a happy ending. When you close — and double lock — the door to your marijuana shop for the last time and hand the keys to its new owner, you will have lived your business's story. It will be a part of you which will never leave you. Make sure it is a story you are proud to tell.

Download Kit

Please enter the URL you see in the box below into your computer web browser to access and download the kit.

---

www.self-counsel.com/updates/srmarijuana/16kit.htm

The download kit includes:

- Business plan template
- Financial worksheets
- Web resources